AF686356

The Power To Create Wealth

31 Biblical principles on prosperity, generosity, contentment, and creating wealth.

Samuel Deuth

Copyright © 2024 by Samuel Deuth

V1.6

Printed in the United States of America | ALL RIGHTS RESERVED No part of this publication may be reproduced, stored in a retrieval system, or transmitted in any form by any means— electronic, mechanical, photocopying, recording, or otherwise— without prior written consent. Scripture quotations, unless otherwise noted, are from The Holy Bible, New International Version ®, NIV ®. Copyright © 1973, 1978, 1984, 2011 by Biblica, Inc. ®

All rights reserved worldwide.

Contents

Contributors

My heartfelt gratitude and thanks to several key business leaders, pastors, mentors, and friends who contributed to this book and interviews from their wealth of experience and revelation on the topic of stewarding and creating wealth from a Biblical perspective.

Thank you to:

Pastor Jurgen Matthesius, Paul Smit, Rabbi Daniel Lapin, Colin Higginbottom, Mark Nelson, Dario Deluca, Marco Contreras, Anthony Trimino, Dr Kevin Dette, Jon Soriano, Zach & Ashley Spear, Cody Cottle, Jim O'Connor, Wes Dunn, Vance Roush, Andre Johnson, Pat Mesiti, and more.

Scan the QR code to watch a powerful range of interviews from the above Kingdom minded industry leaders.

Introduction

For I know the plans I have for you," declares the Lord, "plans to prosper you and not to harm you, plans to give you hope and a future. Jeremiah 29:11 NIV

Wealth is one of the subjects most discussed in the Bible because much of our day-to-day life revolves around money in various ways; how we handle wealth is a window into the condition of our heart. Financial prosperity is not a goal as much as it's an overflow of our heart as we embrace Biblical principles. Now, in life, you're going to have winning and losing seasons, and God may allow us to go through a difficult season to teach and shape us; however, it's not His design for us to struggle and be in lack. He is a provider with a track record of leading His people into blessing and abundance. From providing mana and quail in the wilderness to Jesus feeding the 5,000 from the overflow of a boy's lunch, God is more than enough! Generosity and abundance are his signature.

However, if that's true, why do so many still struggle financially? The two main ways people struggle are lack (poverty) and the love of money (greed). For those reading this book who are in a place of financial struggle, I want you to begin by rejecting the idea that poverty is Godly and embrace the truth of God's good plans for you. And if you're chasing more and more to find purpose, start by rejecting wealth as your source of fulfillment and turn your attention back to God. For those reading this book who are growing your wealth but want to learn more about what the Bible says about the purpose of wealth, lean into the Biblical principles and watch your purpose be ignited and your wealth creation accelerated.

For some of you, talking about money and prosperity is uncomfortable; I pray you find truth and revelation from God's words in these pages. If you embrace Biblical wealth principles, your life will thrive and increase in purpose and impact. Neither my wife Katie nor I came from great wealth, but both came from families that love God and believe that our lives are meant for Kingdom impact. This book contains the principles that have helped my wife and I build from humble beginnings to multiple six figures by applying Biblical wealth-building principles. We've also engaged many experts in a range of industries to extract their wisdom and insight on creating wealth. They are millionaires and billionaires from a wealth standpoint and even more; they are giants in Kingdom building and advancement. When engaged in the right spirit, wealth creation transforms culture and enhances people's lives. As a pastor, I've seen the love of money destroy people, but I've also seen the wonderful impact of those who use their God-given wealth creation ability to make the world a better place. It's God's design for us to use the gold in the ground to benefit others, ourselves, and the broader advancement of The Kingdom of God.

We are blessed to be a blessing!

Samuel Deuth

SECTION 1

Knowing God's Word on Wealth

Do not conform to the pattern of this world, but be transformed by the renewing of your mind. Then you will be able to test and approve what God's will is—his good, pleasing and perfect will.
Romans 12:2 NIV

The most important voice on any topic is its author, designer, originator, and creator; when we engage the topic of money and wealth, we must go straight to the source. We want to allow God's Word to shape our thinking, speaking, and actions related to money and prosperity. I don't want to hang onto old mindsets about wealth that aren't Biblical. I don't want to allow broken and empty secular mindsets about wealth to distort God's intention for our lives. So, whether you're excited about creating wealth or nervous about money being spoken about from a Biblical perspective, I want you to fully open up your heart and mind to God's Word on this topic. As you do, you'll find more purpose, value, enjoyment, and impact than you could ever have imagined. My family, growing up, had an incredible spirit of generosity that came from a biblical mindset. Still, my view of money was often fearful of greed slipping in rather than being focused on the blessing that prosperity can bring to myself and others. So, it was hard to embrace prosperity as being from God and difficult to believe God intended it for our enjoyment. In addition to that, becoming a pastor carries the cultural assumption that ministers should take a vow of poverty and remain broke and poor. So, God had a lot to unwind and rebuild in my wife and my life around wealth. We are now walking in Biblical blessing and prosperity and want to see that in your lives as well. It hasn't been easy; it's been hard fought to unlearn and embrace God's biblical blueprint for prosperity, but it's been rewarding and worth it. So, let's get into this journey of discovering together what the Bible says about the power to create wealth!

Scan to watch our

Wealth Creation Interviews:

Chapter 1

A World of Abundance

The earth is the Lord's, and everything in it, the world, and all who live in it; for he founded it on the seas and established it on the waters. Psalm 24:1-2 NIV

Our godless culture often assumes that resources are scarce and limited, pushing the idea there's not enough to go around. This causes us to compete with others and try to take from others instead of serving them. A lack or scarcity ideology gets us thinking that we increase wealth by transferring it away from others rather than prospering by creating wealth. Abundance and overflow are the nature and character of God. Why would God have created the world with insufficient supply? To receive from God, we must begin to see Him correctly. Do you see God as a stingy tyrant or a kind and generous Father who loves to bless His children? Do you see God as limited or infinite? In the beginning God gave Adam and Eve everything they needed and more. He gave them the best of the land! They had more than enough. Throughout the Bible, we see God blessing and proving Himself to be more than enough for His people. In a book focused on wealth, the first key is to consider what we believe about the one who gives us the power to create wealth. Is Jesus a poor bagger to you? Is Jesus a homeless vagrant who is too lazy to work a real job and lives on handouts and ultimately couldn't save himself from going to the cross? Or do you see Jesus as a humble servant of people who has all authority and established a large ministry team, including a treasurer, that impacted the known world spiritually and politically? And who ultimately became our champion when He put himself on the cross so that his abundance might be transferred to us and our lack be consumed by him. Your heavenly father gave His very best to redeem and rescue us from our own mess and gave us riches for our rags. Yes, those riches, first and foremost, are speaking of spiritual riches that paid the debt of our moral bankruptcy, but the natural blessing, as a rule, follows and flows from spiritual health. You must see God and his purpose for you as overflowing and abundant!

What, then, shall we say in response to these things? If God is for us, who can be against us? He who did not spare his own Son, but gave him up for us all—how will he not also, along with him, graciously give us all things?
Romans 8:31-32 NIV

The Gold is in the Ground

Now the Lord God had planted a garden in the east, in Eden; and there he put the man he had formed. The Lord God made all kinds of trees grow out of the ground—trees that were pleasing to the eye and good for food. In the middle of the garden were the tree of life and the

tree of the knowledge of good and evil. A river watering the garden flowed from Eden; from there it was separated into four headwaters. The name of the first is the Pishon; it winds through the entire land of Havilah, where there is gold. (The gold of that land is good; aromatic resin and onyx are also there.)
Genesis 2:8-12 NIV

Do you believe that a God of abundance would leave you in lack? A big lie from the enemy is, "You aren't able to increase because you don't have the gifting, ability, or resources." But your heavenly Father has created this world and you with everything you need to fulfill your purpose. This was a massive lesson I needed to learn and embrace. It's easier to avoid our responsibility to increase when we take on a disadvantaged victim mindset. But, from the very beginning, God put gold into the ground for Adam and Eve to mine out.

God has equipped you with what you need to prosper.

God gives us what we need to increase. Now, we may need to go and dig it out, but it's there. I was chatting with a friend who was having a hard time identifying additional skills and gifts to make money extra income, feeling like maybe God had shortchanged him; however, as he took time to "dig" into his God-given design, he discovered his passion around the apparel and fashion industry and unlocked a massive future earning potential. Sometimes, our wealth creation abilities are obvious and sometimes more subtle, and often, new streams of income emerge over time and with maturity. When I was young, my family noticed an artistic ability, and I was drawn to get my degree in graphic design, which has served me well over the years. But, along that path, I felt the call to ministry, so I headed in that direction from a career and calling standpoint. As time and skill increased in those areas, I discovered my passion and ability in writing and teaching. I've used all my other talents to fuel that, and together, God has really blessed us, seeing over a dozen books released in multiple languages, reaching and serving millions worldwide!

If you're still questioning whether you have what you need to prosper, I'd encourage you to take the time to pray and seek the input and counsel of others. Often, a third-party perspective gives us insight into fresh ways to create wealth. When I felt stuck over the years, it took a conversation or a seminar-type coaching event to dig up and unlock new gold! In the above scripture, we see that God has intentionally placed in the ground the resources that Adam and Eve needed; he didn't dig it up for them; they had to go and pull out of the earth what they needed. The process of you and I having to dig out the gold causes us to grow and develop dependence not only on God but also on others. We can rarely discover and mine out gold on our own. And the struggle of pulling out resources from the Earth causes us to look deeper at ourselves and our character.

For Katie and I, we've seen seasons of financial difficulty, and blessings expose areas of our hearts that need to be worked on. I remember a time when money was scarce. I didn't know when my next paycheck would come, and my wife had just closed a real estate deal, which brought some financial peace of mind. But, in that, God spoke to me as I went from anxious to peaceful; he said, *"So, now you're at peace when your bank account is full? I need you to be at peace in me before your bank account is good."* Those seasons of lack caused me to see where my trust was really at, whether in God or myself.

Digging out the gold builds and reveals our strengths and weaknesses; it builds the muscles needed to effectively handle wealth when it comes. Like the process a butterfly goes through when breaking out of the cocoon. The breaking-out process provides strength to the wings so they can fly. Don't get frustrated with the process; see it all as God's design and genius. For example, when someone wins big from the lottery but hasn't "struggled to dig out that gold," they don't have the strength to handle it and often end up worse off than before they won. God's genius is to provide both the gold and the ability to dig for it, which shows his generosity and wisdom. I write about these growing seasons in my book, The Process of Promotion.

However, there need be no poor people among you, for in the land the Lord your God is giving you to possess as your inheritance, he will richly bless you, if only you fully obey the Lord your God and are careful to follow all these commands I am giving you today. For the Lord your God will bless you as he has promised, and you will lend to many nations but will borrow from none. You will rule over many nations but none will rule over you. If anyone is poor among your fellow Israelites in any of the towns of the land the Lord your God is giving you, do not be hardhearted or tightfisted toward them. Rather, be openhanded and freely lend them whatever they need. Be careful not to harbor this wicked thought: "The seventh year, the year for canceling debts, is near," so that you do not show ill will toward the needy among your fellow Israelites and give them nothing. They may then appeal to the Lord against you, and you will be found guilty of sin.
Deuteronomy 15:4-9 NIV

The Gold Is Good

The gold of that land is good; aromatic resin and onyx are also there. Genesis 2:8-12 NIV

It's important to note how the Bible speaks of something the first time it's mentioned, and right from the beginning, God calls gold GOOD. He's pointing out and noting the specific location of high-quality gold. He doesn't say anything about staying away from it because money is evil; instead, he's saying to go after the finest and most precious resource on earth. Some of you, like myself, need to start by reframing your idea about money; if God made it, placed it in the ground, called it good, and told us where to get the best, then that's how we need to see and think about wealth.

It's available and it's good.

Prosperity is a Sign of God's Presence

I will cleanse them from all the sin they have committed against me and will forgive all their sins of rebellion against me. Then this city will bring me renown, joy, praise and honor before all nations on earth that hear of all the good things I do for it; and they will be in awe and will tremble at the abundant prosperity and peace I provide for it.'
Jeremiah 33:8-9 NIV

As you read through the Bible, you'll see this theme: when God blessed and was with someone, they prospered, increased, and multiplied. Often in culture, the devil has been good at painting the idea that when you're wealthy it's because you cheated others or you're motivated only by greed, and while that may be the case for some, the Bible consistently describes the opposite picture; when God is with His nation or an individual they increase, prosper and are in health.

As children of God, ours is the best of the land! Don't assume God wants you to just survive and scrape by, God wants you to enjoy. He placed Adam and Eve in the middle of the garden with the best of what the land offered. The devil is the one from the beginning trying to get them to doubt the goodness and provision of God. Claiming, "Did God really say?" You'll find that's the same accusing spirit trying to get believers to doubt God's good plans and intension for them. We must trust and grab hold of God's Word, knowing that when we live His principles who we'll produce his fruits.

When you live out Bible principles you'll get Bible results.
Pastor Leanne Matthesius

Chapter 2

God is Our Provider

And my God will liberally supply (fill until full) your every need according to His riches in glory in Christ Jesus.
Philippians 4:19 Amplified Bible

While traveling to Israel a few years ago, I was chatting with a young Jewish man who was training in the schools in Jerusalem. We talked about different Jewish traditions, he said that before they eat, they don't say a traditional prayer as I might do over the meal, but they say a phrase similar to this;

Eloheinu melekh ha'olam hamotzi lehem min ha'aretz.

This means, Blessed are You, Lord our God, Ruler of the universe, who brings forth bread from the earth. The man clarified it as meaning, "Everything comes from you." I love that, and it's a great ongoing reminder that we are not the source of provision but that all things come from God. The Bible says that God makes things grow; we plant seeds, but it's God who makes them grow. James says that every good and perfect gift comes from above. In Acts 17, it says that in Him we live and move and have our being. He is the creator and giving of all things. Even the power to create wealth comes from Him. More specifically, your DNA, personality, and skills have been hardwired by God into your life. We mine out those skills and gifts, but we didn't make those genetic skills possible. It all comes from God and is given by him. The sooner we begin to see that all things come from God and that we are simply stewards of it, the more effectively we'll multiply and use wealth. As a parent, I give my kids stewardship over their room, but all they have is from me. This also means that I require them to manage what I've given them well. God created the garden, placed people in it, and commanded them to work and expand it. God has given us a trust and a responsibility to extend what we have beyond it.

So Abraham called that place The Lord Will Provide. And to this day it is said, "On the mountain of the Lord it will be provided." Genesis 22:14 NIV

Years ago, when I was on a mission trip to Africa, God gave me a greater revelation about the story of Abraham and his testing. It ends with the revelation about God being Jehovah Jireh, God our Provider. The Bible says, "on the mountain of the Lord, it will be provided." This would be a foreshadowing of Jesus providing salvation in the future, and it lets us know that you find God's provision on the path of obedience to God's will. When I submit my life, work, business, ministry, family, and all aspects of my life in obedience to His will, we'll always cross paths with God's provision.

Humility is the fear of the Lord; its wages are riches and honor and life. Proverbs 22:4 NIV

Partnering with The Holy Spirit

The Israelites sampled their provisions
but did not inquire of the Lord.
Joshua 9:14 NIV

From a general business point of view, you make all your work and investment moves based on a careful inspection of the present data and some gut instincts; most of the time, that will work. But there are times when we don't always see underneath the surface of the deal, and that's when we must learn to consistently engage with and respond to the guidance of the Holy Spirit. The above verse from Joshua powerfully illustrates bad business deals that can happen when we make all our investing and financial decisions based solely on the natural data we can see. The Bible says the Holy Spirit is our comforter, guide, and counselor. Not only does God give wisdom and direction, but he also protects, shields, and brings supernatural favor. We must invite Him to speak and guide us in our business and wealth-creation strategies. Are we praying in the spirit? Are we pausing to get quiet and allow Him to talk to us? There were several investing opportunities when I was younger that I jumped on without really taking time to ask God if he was in it or not, and many of them ended up losing big. While there may always be some risks involved in creating wealth, there are many insights that God can provide if we take the time to stop and listen.

Regarding the books I write, I'm always leaning in to ask God what the next book I need to write is. Sometimes, I may want to jump on a particular topic, but I don't sense God's Amen. For this current book, I wasn't sure when the right timing was; I've been feeling it for a while now, and in prayer and Bible reading, it felt like all words were pointing toward making the topic of Biblical Wealth Creation the next book. As I began to write, it began to flow quickly because it was the right book for the right time.

The greatest competitive business advantage I have is Christ.
Mark Nelson
Commercial Real Estate Investor

In addition to seeking God's insight to ensure we're prosperous, it's imperative to stay leaning into His voice and His Word to make sure our work is aligned with God's Word and is effectively establishing His Kingdom. Like Jesus' statement, "We want to be about our Father's business." While God has given us a broad mandate to take dominion on the earth, and we're given freedom within that call, we don't want to be trying to get God to bless "our actions" when we should be choosing to do what God is blessing. We should commit to bringing Glory to God through our lives and work.

So whether you eat or drink or whatever you do,
do it all for the glory of God.
1 Corinthians 10:31 NIV

Trust God or Riches?

He who leans on and trusts in and is confident in his riches will fall,

But the righteous [who trust in God's provision] will flourish like a green leaf.
Proverbs 11:28 AMP

God is who we put our trust in. God is stable and constant—a foundation we can put our hope and trust in. Money, government, and economies may fail us, but God will never fail or leave you. Money is a facilitator, but it's not a great foundation. When you lean on money, you will fall, but when you lean on God and trust Him, money will help you facilitate God's purposes!

How abundant are the good things that you have stored up for those who fear you, that you bestow in the sight of all, on those who take refuge in you.
Psalms 31:19 NIV

Getting a Word from God

Then Caleb silenced the people before Moses and said, "We should go up and take possession of the land, for we can certainly do it."
Numbers 13:30 NIV

In Numbers 13, we see the story of the 12 spies who went to check out the promised land. Ten came back with a negative report. You can tell Caleb is shocked by the report being given to the people, and he jumps in and says, "We can certainly do it." Why would he say that? How did he know that? Because God had already promised that He would give them the city. As a people, they had already been given a prophetic word through Moses about taking the land. So, while everyone else was afraid because of the size of the Jericho walls, Caleb and Joshua held on to the strength of the Word from God.

In the same way, before you step out into a new venture, stop and take time to get a word from God for the battles ahead. When you face giants and walls, you need something from which to draw strength. When my wife and I moved from Seattle to San Diego in 2015, it was a massive faith leap: little savings and no job. We were stepping out into freelance, entrepreneurial, and itinerate ministry work. There were many difficult nights and months in those beginning years; a few times, we wondered if we would make it. But, in those difficult times, our best weapon was to go back to the Words from God that we got along the way to affirm and confirm that we were called to make the move. There were several specific words from God telling us to move to San Diego, step out in itinerate ministry, and more. We got one word that said, "This move will be more difficult than you think." Now, that might not sound encouraging, but when things got tough, it was an encouraging reminder that we were on the right track, so we didn't give up. Whether you're starting your own business, planting a church, taking on a new position at your job, or whatever the next step may be, lean into the Bible, The Holy Spirit, and trusted believers to seek God's Word; it will be a weapon for you in the heat of the battle!

They were helped in fighting them, and God delivered the Hagrites and all their allies into their hands, because they cried out to him during the battle. He answered their prayers, because they trusted in him.
1 Chronicles 5:20 NIV

Chapter 3

Biblical Prosperity

The blessing of the Lord brings [true] riches, And He adds no sorrow to it [for it comes as a blessing from God].
Proverbs 10:22 Amplified Bible

Jabez was more honorable than his brothers. His mother had named him Jabez, saying, "I gave birth to him in pain." Jabez cried out to the God of Israel, "Oh, that you would bless me and enlarge my territory! Let your hand be with me, and keep me from harm so that I will be free from pain." And God granted his request.
1 Chronicles 4:9-10 NIV

Wealth and prosperity can be complex topics simply because we all define rich and poor differently. We may describe someone as "wealthy" at different income levels. One might say if you have 10k in the bank, you're wealthy, while others might not qualify you as rich until you reach multiple millions in net worth. Because the Bible is true for all people at all times and in all nations, there is no specific dollar amount that the Bible labels rich. It's true that the true riches of the Kingdom are not wealth; rather, true wealth is salvation, relationship with God, and eternity secured. So, while the topic of prosperity as a follower of Jesus includes natural and eternal rewards, this book focuses more on what the Bible says about creating monetary wealth and the purpose, use, and impact of financial wealth and prosperity. How we handle the natural wealth impacts how God trusts us with spiritual wealth. Also, how we handle natural wealth is spiritual because God looks to see how we steward all He has given us.

So if you have not been trustworthy in handling worldly wealth, who will trust you with true riches?
Luke 16:11 NIV

For this book, our working definition of Biblical prosperity or poverty is based on overflow or lack of. I love how my pastor, Jurgen Matthesius, defined Biblical prosperity.

To be biblically poor is to have less than you need for your own bills and no extra to help others. To be rich is to have all that you need for your expenses and to have extra to serve others.

This definition is excellent because it works in every nation and every generation. Whether you're in New York or Tanzania, Africa, you can aim to create and grow your wealth until you're prosperous enough to have what you need and overflow to care for others. There's nothing virtuous about being poor because it limits our ability to serve others.

The rich rule over the poor, and the borrower is slave to the lender.
Proverbs 22:7 NIV

How do you see money?

Both riches and honor come from You, and You rule over all. In Your hand is power and might; and it is in Your hands to make great and to give strength to everyone.
1 Chronicles 29:12 Amplified Bible

We must first ask ourselves how we see God and then how we see money. We know that the Bible says that wealth, honor, and prosperity come from the Lord. So, wealth can't be an evil thing because everything that flows from God is good; He wouldn't promise the reward of wealth if it was evil. We have to learn to see correctly, or we won't engage with money properly. The primary purpose of this book is to help you see what God says about creating, having, and using wealth. How we engage money will reflect our view of God. Do you see God as big, giving, kind, generous, compassionate, generational, and legacy-minded? If so, then your money should be focused in the same way. People with a small view of God are typically stingy and live small. People who see the world God made as limited and scarce will tend to clutch tightly all they have because they fear that the world is running out of resources. But the infinite and unlimited God did not create a limited world. God wants you to be an echo of Him in this world, living big and generous toward others.

Business Is God's Idea

Allow God to shape your idea of prosperity rather than assuming culture's definition. I love how Rabbi Daniel Lapin provides insight in his book, Business Secrets of The

Bible (which I highly recommend.)

Wealth is God's incentive to serve others.
Rabbi Daniel Lapin
Author & Business Coach

Rabbi Lapin shares that The Biblical definition of a Businessman is being a man of faith because it requires trust in God to sow, build, and create something out of nothing. I love how he points out that God designed the essence of business and commerce to serve others; when we serve others better, we get more significant compensation. So, God designed the world and commerce to work best when we are less self-indulgent, and more service-focused. Business is serving the needs of others; life rewards you when you do good to others. The more good you do for people, the greater your business will grow! Rabbi Lapin also points out that the Hebrew language has no word for "win." In the sense of winning unearned money. We don't "win" money; we earn or create it through business. The exchange of goods or services is business. The more we serve each other, the more wealth is created, and we literally grow the economy this way. Money multiplies in business. For example, if you're a furniture maker. You are serving the customer who is requesting the chair. But then you're adding value to the company making the screws and wood you're using to make the chair. You're making wealth from serving people who need a chair, and in the process, you're creating value for the metal worker and lumbar yard.

With my books and resources. God gave me ideas for resources that serve others; I created those with God's help and then brought them to the market. I'm adding value to churches and, in turn, receiving value. We're expanding the economy and serving each other. My publisher is winning, the companies producing the paper are winning, the churches are winning, and new believers are being discipled.

We create wealth by serving others.

Chapter 4

Sowing and Reaping

As long as the earth endures, seedtime and harvest, cold and heat, summer and winter, day and night will never cease.
Genesis 8:22 NIV

God established principles by which the world operates and flows. One of those foundational principles is sowing and reaping. God created the world to work in seasons. Seasons of planting, seasons of waiting(development), seasons of reaping. We cannot expect from one season if we haven't properly invested in the previous. Because of the sowing and reaping principles, you can approach life with the expectation that your planting will be rewarded. Take a moment to evaluate your life; are you in a planting, waiting, or harvest season? A farmer acts differently in each season. If you need to see a harvest and you're not seeing it, it's time to plant again in this current field or identify new fields.

Sluggards do not plow in season;
so at harvest time they look but find nothing.
Proverbs 20:4 NIV

This verse and principle from Proverbs is vital:

don't look for a harvest you didn't plant. Too many are frustrated because they don't see a harvest in one area or another, but if we're honest, we often haven't sown the seed for that harvest. However, if we have sown and aren't seeing the harvest yet, then we have to learn to be patient in the process of development. I wrote more extensively about this in my book *The Process of Promotion.*

Better a little with the fear of the Lord than great wealth with turmoil. Better a small serving of vegetables with love than a fattened calf with hatred.
Proverbs 15:16-17 NIV

Season vs. Ruts

One of the more helpful revelations that kickstarted our journey from lack to abundance came during a conversation with our friend Dr. Matt Hubbard. We were talking about the state of our finances, and we said, "It's just a season we're in; things will change if we keep at it." He asked, "How long has it been this way?" Embarrassingly, we said, "About 14 years!" He then said, that's not a season; that's a rut! At the time, it was a sobering thought, but it shook me loose from being okay with rut-living. Consider the length of a regular season; it's about three or four months, so if we've been in a season for a few years, we're not just in a season; we're in a rut and need to work on making changes to break out of the ditch.

Now, how do you know if you're just in the "waiting" season? That's a legitimate question since we often get impatient with the hidden and challenging seasons. Here's how I check to see if it's a rut or the waiting season.

First, I'm praying and asking God for insight, checking to see if I'm missing something in the circumstance that God's trying to speak to me about. If God isn't keeping you in the season, then my next step is to seek the wisdom and counsel of trusted friends, pastors, leaders, parents, or mentors who can assess if you're stuck or planted. If you're stuck, it won't produce; if you're planted, it will be dark for a while before you emerge into the sunlight. Usually, mentors who are beyond you have already seen your stage of the journey, so they can quickly diagnose and offer feedback.

Wealth creation has more to do with behavior than it does intellect. You do not need to be smart financially to make a lot of money. You just need to have the right behavior.
Jim O'Connor | Wealth Investment Coach

My area of expertise has been in ministry leadership, so when I'd visit a church and minister, I could quickly tell why the church was or wasn't growing since my church leadership experience was beyond that pastor's experience or stage of their church. In the same way, when we felt stuck in our financial difficulty, it seemed like it was overwhelming, but for others beyond us, they weren't nervous. It's helpful to keep yourself around people who have killed great giants so that your giants feel small to them. Then, they can help you conquer. When you're in the middle of your rut, it seems way too challenging to get out of it, but others can easily guide you through if you're willing to allow them to. Don't let pride, arrogance, and insecurity turn a season into a rut. I remember feeling embarrassed about my financial situation, but I faced my issues head-on and fully embraced all the wisdom coming my way.

Chapter 5

Power to Create Wealth

But remember the Lord your God, for it is he who gives you the ability to produce wealth, and so confirms his covenant, which he swore to your ancestors, as it is today.
Deuteronomy 8:18 NIV

Do not trust in extortion or put vain hope in stolen goods; though your riches increase, do not set your heart on them. One thing God has spoken, two things I have heard: "Power belongs to you, God, and with you, Lord, is unfailing love"; and, "You reward everyone according to what they have done."
Psalms 62:10-12 NIV

The source of life, increase, and favor is God himself. When we begin to work on creating wealth and increase, it's not separate from God and his Word, but rather, it flows out from being connected to the source of life. God said that the gold in the ground is very good, and from the beginning, God called us to draw rich resources out of the ground. God blessed Adam and Eve and gave them a mandate to increase, multiply, and take dominion.

Work is not a byproduct of sin entering the earth; work is a gift from God that blesses humanity. Work provides purpose, value, and meaning for ourselves, and work is about serving others. Gold is a reward for that work and service to others. With the commonly held feeling that money is dirty or the source of evil, it's hard to receive from God what he wants to give us. Not only is prospering not evil, but it's actually the overflow of doing good. God is the source of all things; He is our provider and gives us the ability to produce good things. God is a creator, and we are created in His image, so it makes sense that we are called and empowered to create. Not only are we empowered to create wealth, but we're responsible and expected to do it. We're called to bear fruit that will last. One of the common things that we get wrong as believers is that we assume that trusting God or being empowered to create wealth means that we sit back and wait for God to do it. Sometimes, it's out of laziness and often out of a wrong view of faith.

God used a concept from T. Harv Ekcr's book, The Millionaire Mind, to wake me up to the truth of our role in wealth creation. He said, "Wealthy people take full responsibility for their financial success." This may seem simple, but up until reading that, I had subconsciously been waiting on God to "bless me" but not realizing that God had given me the power to create wealth. I was waiting on God to do something, and I learned as I studied the scriptures with fresh eyes that God had already empowered me; now, I just needed to get after it. I realized that if I wasn't prospering, it wasn't because God was holding me back but because I was not stepping into the role I needed as the wealth creator God had called me to be. Taking full responsibility for wealth creation was a phrase that shifted a lot for me. The Holy Spirit highlighted scriptures confirming our role in wealth production. Through the parable of the talents, God showed me that while He gave the talents, it wasn't by accident that they multiplied their wealth. The man who went from two talents to four and the one who went from five talents to ten didn't stumble into wealth creation; they took responsibility for what God had given them and multiplied it. It takes intention and strategy.

Obedience Produces Prosperity

Deuteronomy 8 shows that prosperity is a sign of God being with you. Yes, you read that right; the spiritual is revealed in the natural. When God's supernatural blessing is on someone, it materializes in the natural. Ironically, we as a culture love to celebrate the Biblical qualities of humility, diligence, and stewardship but then condemn and judge those same people when their Biblical way of living produces wealth and honor. Make a decision to live out the Biblical principles and always celebrate the rewards of righteousness God brings to others. Never curse publicly or in your heart the blessing of God on others or yourself. Take a look at just a few of the verses in Deuteronomy 28 where God is telling His people how He promises to bless them when they fully obey Him:

If you fully obey the Lord your God and carefully follow all his commands I give you today, the Lord your God will set you high above all the nations on earth. All these blessings will come on you and accompany you if you obey the Lord your God: You will be blessed in the city and blessed in the country. The fruit of your womb will be blessed, and the crops of your land and the young of your livestock—

the calves of your herds and the lambs of your flocks. Your basket and your kneading trough will be blessed. You will be blessed when you come in and blessed when you go out. The Lord will grant that the enemies who rise up against you will be defeated before you. They will come at you from one direction but flee from you in seven. The Lord will send a blessing on your barns and on everything you put your hand to. The Lord your God will bless you in the land he is giving you. The Lord will establish you as his holy people, as he promised you on oath, if you keep the commands of the Lord your God and walk in obedience to him. Then all the peoples on earth will see that you are called by the name of the Lord, and they will fear you. The Lord will grant you abundant prosperity—in the fruit of your womb, the young of your livestock and the crops of your ground—in the land he swore to your ancestors to give you.
Deuteronomy 28:1-11 NIV

Blessing follows obedience. God is a rewarder! I'm hammering these statements because I know it took me a while to thoroughly examine and embrace these truths. What we sow, we will reap. He is a rewarder of those who diligently seek Him.

Partnering with God

In the course of time, David inquired of the Lord. "Shall I go up to one of the towns of Judah?" he asked. The Lord said, "Go up." David asked, "Where shall I go?" "To Hebron," the Lord answered.
2 Samuel 2:1 NIV

Before business moves, seek God – Don't get into battles or business if God isn't in it. God is the creator of all the raw materials and the giver of the raw gifts and talents that you have within you, but now it's our privilege and responsibility to mine gold from the earth and from ourselves. Notice how Jesus speaks into the fishing industry with supernatural insight.

When he had finished speaking, he said to Simon, "Put out into deep water, and let down the nets for a catch." Simon answered, "Master, we've worked hard all night and haven't caught anything. But because you say so, I will let down the nets." When they had done so, they caught such a large number of fish that their nets began to break. So they signaled their partners in the other boat to come and help them, and they came and filled both boats so full that they began to sink. When Simon Peter saw this, he fell at Jesus' knees and said, "Go away from me, Lord; I am a sinful man!
Luke 5:4-8 NIV

God doesn't always guide us in unconventional faith moves in our business, but when He does, be ready to lean in and respond. There's always a miracle on the other side of crazy faith. Not only does God want to partner with you to grow your business, but He'll also invite you to submit your business to the service of Kingdom Business. The story we read above is beautiful because, before the supernatural catch, Peter offered the "platform" of his boat and business to Jesus to speak to the crowds. Partnering with God brings greater purpose and prosperity to our lives.

Heaven Doesn't Do Welfare

The day after the Passover, that very day, they ate some of the produce of the land: unleavened bread and roasted grain. The manna stopped the day after they ate this food from the land; there was no longer any manna for the Israelites, but that year they ate the produce of Canaan. Joshua 5:11-12 NIV

It's so powerful to notice that God's supernatural provision carried them through uniquely difficult times, but God's desire was to bring them into a blessed land where they would work, cultivate, and produce. We often think we need to work hard to get to the place where it all comes easy, and while God's promises of abundance will come with grace, it's not a handout for free. In our faith move from Seattle to San Diego, like mentioned, the initial seasons were difficult financially. In those initial months, there were two major supernatural provision moments. One time, God prompted someone to send hundreds of dollars worth of groceries to our home just when we needed it most. And another time, God prompted my brother and sister-in-law, Stephen and Amanda Deuth, to send us a check in the mail; little did they know it was the exact amount of money we were short that month. Those were beautiful supernatural provision moments that confirmed and affirmed God's presence, calling, and goodness in our lives for the season. But then I felt God speak to me and say, now it's time to produce. God's optimal desire is that we're in a wealth creation state not a handout state. God will supernaturally carry you when needed, and sometimes bless us to show his favor, but His goal is always to move you into a place of abundance.

All hard work brings a profit, but mere talk leads only to poverty. The wealth of the wise is their crown, but the folly of fools yields folly. Proverbs 14:23-24 NIV

Chapter 6

Generosity & Greed

Many Christians who are nervous about the topic of money attempt to quote the Bible by saying that money is the root of evil. This idea is a misquote of the Bible and often an excuse, if we're honest, for our lack of financial blessing. When we read the Bible, we see many honored Biblical characters who are incredibly wealthy, so let's look at what the Bible actually says:

For the love of money is a root of all kinds of evil. Some people, eager for money, have wandered from the faith and pierced themselves with many griefs.
1 Timothy 6:10 NIV

The Bible says the "love" of money is "a" root. Money itself is not good or bad; its power is in the place we give it. When money isn't in its correct place, it has a way of tripping us up and pulling us off track. We love God and make money our servant; we don't love money and try to make God our servant. Money is an amplifier of what's in our hearts.

No one can serve two masters. Either you will hate the one and love

the other, or you will be devoted to the one and despise the other. You cannot serve both God and money.
Matthew 6:24 NIV

If we serve and worship God, money will help us serve and positively impact more people. If we allow greed and selfish living to lead us, we'll use and control people to get money. The truth is that many have used or been used by money to control and manipulate people and use wealth in addictive and self-destructive ways. It's essential to allow God to search our hearts and deal with the places of our hearts that aren't surrendered to him. We must boldly declare that we will not worship money; we'll worship God and make money serve us and the purposes of God.

The greedy bring ruin to their households,
but the one who hates bribes will live.
Proverbs 15:27 NIV

Especially in the culture and time we're writing this book, where much of the focus on money is self-gratifying and self-serving rather than Kingdom-minded and others-focused. When pursuing wealth causes a lack of health in other areas of your life, you have started to make that your god rather than serving God. You'll know when you're serving God because it will bring life to you and all those around you. In contrast, when you've made money, your god, it will bring death to you and all those around you. The love of money and greed are killers and cannot produce the life we desire! Being on guard against greed means being ready and intentional in resisting greed's attempt to take us out.

Then he said to them, "Watch out! Be on your guard against all kinds of greed; life does not consist in an abundance of possessions." And he told them this parable: "The ground of a certain rich man yielded an abundant harvest. He thought to himself, 'What shall I do? I have no place to store my crops.' "Then he said, 'This is what I'll do. I will tear down my barns and build bigger ones, and there I will store my surplus grain. And I'll say to myself, "You have plenty of grain laid up for many years. Take life easy; eat, drink and be merry."' "But God said to him, 'You fool! This very night your life will be demanded from you. Then who will get what you have prepared for yourself?' "This is how it will be with whoever stores up things for themselves but is not rich toward God.
Luke 12:15-21 NIV

Greed leads you to mistreat people. To create unnecessary conflict. It clouds our judgment and hinders our ability to see the gold in people. It ends up blocking you from the very thing you're seeking. You'll notice that greed often instigates conflict with others in your life.

The greedy stir up conflict, but those who trust in the Lord will prosper. Those who trust in themselves are fools, but those who walk in wisdom are kept safe. Those who give to the poor will lack nothing, but those who close their eyes to them receive many curses.
Proverbs 28:25-27 NIV

The Antidote to Greed

One person gives freely, yet gains even more; another withholds unduly, but comes to poverty. A generous person will prosper; whoever refreshes others will be refreshed.
Proverbs 11:24-25 NIV

Does money or the love of money have a way of destroying people? Absolutely! This is why we must be wise about how it can creep in and choke us out. This whole book provides the balance of this idea in tandem with wealth-building principles. But I've discovered a simple way of keeping greed at bay; giving. Christians are commonly nervous about falling into the trap of greed, but remember that generosity is the greatest antidote to greed.

Greedy people don't give, and giving people don't greed.
Jurgen Matthesius

The stingy person's world keeps shrinking, but a generous person's world expands and multiplies! Keep your eyes and attention on giving and serving, and you'll never have to worry about the love of wealth taking root in your heart. One of the ways this shows up is in tithes and offering moments in church. Especially the offerings that are above your regular tithe. How easily can you and I release an offering? How much do you white-knuckle-grip your wealth? How easily can you sow it and give it? Usually, when people get offended at a church, "just wanting my money," it's a sign they have greed in their hearts or a lack and poverty mentality. If you are generous, you'll look for chances to sow, give, and bless others and the Kingdom of God; if you're greedy and stingy, every call to generosity will offend you.

A Transformed Heart is Generous

But Zacchaeus stood up and said to the Lord, "Look, Lord! Here and now, I give half of my possessions to the poor, and if I have cheated

anybody out of anything, I will pay back four times the amount." Jesus said to him, "Today salvation has come to this house, because this man, too, is a son of Abraham. For the Son of Man came to seek and to save the lost.
Luke 19:8-10 NIV

The story of a greedy tax collector who turned into a wildly generous man is a model of how we should respond when we encounter salvation through Jesus. When our heart encounters the generosity of heaven, it should then make a similar shift towards generosity. People who claim to be Christians but have a hard time being generous with money need to seek God for the answer as to why they have a stingy heart when God has been so over-the-top kind to them. If you find it difficult to be generous, I encourage you to spend more time meditating on the goodness and kindness of God. Allow His love to fill every part of your heart so you live in an overflowing state. Appreciating God's generosity will cause you to level up and be more at ease with releasing money in tithing, offerings, and benevolence.

Sacrifice > Amount

Jesus sat down opposite the place where the offerings were put and watched the crowd putting their money into the temple treasury. Many rich people threw in large amounts. But a poor widow came and put in two very small copper coins worth only a few cents. Calling his disciples to him, Jesus said, "Truly I tell you, this poor widow has put more into the treasury than all the others. They all gave out of their wealth; but she, out of her poverty, put in everything—all she had to live on.
Mark 12:41-44 NIV

Jesus showcases the importance of tithes, offerings, and generosity by observing people giving and honoring the one in the room who gave the most significant percentage of her wealth, not just the largest amount. Jesus honors sacrifice, so is your generosity growing as your income rises? Are you being sacrificially generous? It doesn't matter that you give a lot; it matters what it costs you to give that amount. Over the years, I've had entrepreneurs start explaining to me why they aren't giving right now. They'll usually try to suggest that once they break into a higher earning level, they'll begin to tithe and give offerings, and I've learned to challenge that and say, "No, you won't." Why would I be that harsh? Because generosity is a heart posture, if it's not present when you have little, it sure won't show up when you're wealthy. Be faithful and generous with little, and God will give you much. Recently, my friend Nick Ryan was encouraging our church on giving; he echoed the above and said he used to think, "I'll tithe when I start making more money," but God said, "No, you won't. How you handle little is how you'll handle much. If you can't be faithful with the tithe now, you won't later." He went on to share that his now wife, Katie, said, "I won't marry a man who robs God." Needless to say, he got in alignment with God's Word, and he and his wife are some of the most blessed and generous people we know!

Chapter 7

Called to Multiply

One of the most descriptive examples in the Bible of what God expects from us is a parable Jesus shares called the Parable of the Talents or the Parable of the Bags of Gold. It shows God's expectation of what we've been given. Have you considered the idea that your generous heavenly Father has some expectations about what we do? You'll see we're called to multiply what we've been given. Let's take the time to read through the entire parable and draw a few notes.

Again, it will be like a man going on a journey, who called his servants and entrusted his wealth to them. To one he gave five bags of gold, to another two bags, and to another one bag, each according to his ability. Then he went on his journey. The man who had received five bags of gold went at once and put his money to work and gained five bags more. So also, the one with two bags of gold gained two more. But the man who had received one bag went off, dug a hole in the ground and hid his master's money. "After a long time, the master of those servants returned and settled accounts with them. The man who had received five bags of gold brought the other five. 'Master,' he said, 'you entrusted me with five bags of gold. See, I have gained five more.' "His master replied, 'Well done, good and faithful servant! You have been faithful

with a few things; I will put you in charge of many things. Come and share your master's happiness!' "The man with two bags of gold also came. 'Master,' he said, 'you entrusted me with two bags of gold; see, I have gained two more.' "His master replied, 'Well done, good and faithful servant! You have been faithful with a few things; I will put you in charge of many things. Come and share your master's happiness!' "Then the man who had received one bag of gold came. 'Master,' he said, 'I knew that you are a hard man, harvesting where you have not sown and gathering where you have not scattered seed. So I was afraid and went out and hid your gold in the ground. See, here is what belongs to you.' "His master replied, 'You wicked, lazy servant! So you knew that I harvest where I have not sown and gather where I have not scattered seed? Well then, you should have put my money on deposit with the bankers, so that when I returned I would have received it back with interest. "'So take the bag of gold from him and give it to the one who has ten bags. For whoever has will be given more, and they will have an abundance. Whoever does not have, even what they have, will be taken from them. And throw that worthless servant outside, into the darkness, where there will be weeping and gnashing of teeth.'
Matthew 25:14-30 NIV

Notice that Jesus gives different amounts of money to the three individuals; God gives us resources proportional to our ability. Some of that ability is God-given, and some is grown by us. God isn't concerned with giving each person the same amount of money because he doesn't require an equal amount in return, but equal effort and multiplication based on their ability and what He gave them. The one servant who only saved his money and didn't grow it was condemned as lazy. So, we are responsible not just for maintaining what we've been given, but we have a mandate to multiply!

Another thing, when the master leaves the employees, he doesn't give them an exact amount they must increase by; he just gives them resources and says I'll settle up the account when I return. This is how God sees each of us. He's given you and me talents and the power to create wealth. When we die or when he returns, whichever happens first, there will be a moment where we come before Him and give him an accounting of what he gave us and what we did with it. Will we squander it? Will we sit on it? Or will we follow the wise servant examples by putting our resources to work and multiplying what we've been given?

Blessing and Multiplication

and none of the condemned things are to be found in your hands. Then the Lord will turn from his fierce anger, will show you mercy, and will have compassion on you. He will increase your numbers, as he promised on oath to your ancestors—
Deuteronomy 13:17 NIV

Notice that the blessing of God and multiplication go hand in hand. Growth, increase, and multiplication are the fruit and byproduct of God being with you. While there will be rest seasons, winter seasons, and testing seasons where the fruit and increase aren't visible or delayed, the ultimate end of God being on something is for it to increase, expand, and multiply. The original mandate from God was to increase and multiply and to fill the earth. Living small is not your design. You're hardwired by God to take territory.

Clear & Conquer

But Joshua said to the tribes of Joseph—to Ephraim and Manasseh—"You are numerous and very powerful. You will have not only one allotment but the forested hill country as well. Clear it, and its farthest limits will be yours; though the Canaanites have chariots fitted with iron and though they are strong, you can drive them out.
Joshua 17:17-18 NIV

The tribe of Manasseh was complaining that they didn't have enough land. Joshua tells them, you have land, but you're unwilling to take possession of it because of fear, laziness, or fatigue. They wanted land they didn't have to battle so hard for. If we want the land, God will need us to "clear" some things and "Conquer" some things. Multiplication, as we've already mentioned, isn't automatic. It will require blood, sweat, and tears to see the increase. The Bible says that Godly wealth comes without sorrow, not without work. The promise is that when God adds to your life, it brings peace, but money will come with pain and anxiety if you're striving for it.

Take Dominion

Then God blessed them, and God said to them, "Be fruitful and multiply; fill the earth and subdue it; have dominion over the fish of the sea, over the birds of the air, and over every living thing that moves on the earth.
Genesis 1:28 (NKJV)

How do you see yourself and your role on earth? Some see themselves as randomly placed here with no purpose. Some may see themselves as unwelcome intruders on the earth. When we don't see ourselves with God-given authority to take dominion, we tend to be more intimidated and shrink back from going after the territory that God has given us. You are here to establish God's kingdom on earth and build cities and nations. Don't settle for less than your promised land. It's important to note that I'm not talking about the never-satisfied spirit in culture, which always needs or wants more. I'm talking about stepping into what you've been given. God gave certain lands, regions, and places for his people to go. We're to take dominion in the space He's called us into. Establishing the Kingdom of God will also drive a healthy and right spirit around wealth creation. Being dominion-minded gives your wealth vision, boundaries, and purpose. Many get off track when they solely focus on building their own kingdom rather than advancing the cause of Christ.

God has given us both the responsibility and authority to rule and oversee the earth.

SECTION 2

The Purpose and Enjoyment of Wealth

Command those who are rich in this present world not to be arrogant nor to put their hope in wealth, which is so uncertain, but to put their hope in God, who richly provides us with everything for our enjoyment. Command them to do good, to be rich in good deeds, and to be generous and willing to share.
1 Timothy 6:17-18 NIV

What was and is God's intended way for us to handle money and wealth? Is wealth only about others? Is it wrong to enjoy your prosperity? Should you feel guilty if you get too wealthy? Should you only keep just what you need to cover your bills? Various perspectives surround what God says about how Christians, and people in general, should engage money. At the time of this writing, there are a couple of main negative ideas around money, for example, that having "too much" money is evil or that any "excessive" enjoyment when others have less is ungodly. The idea in those circles might be that God wants you to just have enough for yourself. The common idea in movies is that Christians, especially pastors and church leaders, should take a vow of poverty. In other circles, which I'd be a part of, we see wealth as a sign of the blessing of God on right living. We see the world and its resources as something to be enjoyed. So, does God want you to enjoy your life? Does he want you to have nice things and enjoy recreation and vacations, or does he want you to give away all wealth, live just barely above poverty, and renounce all enjoyment and pleasure? Let's dive deeper into what God's Word says about the purpose and enjoyment of wealth.

Scan to watch our
Wealth Creation Interviews:

Chapter 8

Return to the Garden

The Lord God took the man and put him in the Garden of Eden to work it and take care of it. And the Lord God commanded the man, "You are free to eat from any tree in the garden; but you must not eat from the tree of the knowledge of good and evil, for when you eat from it you will certainly die.
Genesis 2:15-17 NIV

Let's look to the beginning of creation to see a glimpse of God's original intent for humanity. The Bible says God gave everything to Adam and Eve for them to work and enjoy. Nothing was off limits to them. There was no command to deny themselves of the fruit, beauty, gold, or anything else of the Land. The only thing that God made off-limits was the tree in the middle of the garden. That was to be a way for humanity to choose to submit and honor God and give back to God. Not only did God create beauty, but He put Adam and Eve right in the middle of the best! He held nothing back from them, and God holds nothing back from us today. The earth and all goodness and beauty are yours and available to you. Are there boundaries and limits to self-indulgence? Yes, but within God's moral boundaries is free range of the best of the Land!

Favored Children

May those who delight in my vindication shout for joy and gladness; may they always say, "The Lord be exalted, who delights in the well-being of his servant.
Psalm 35:27 NIV

However, as it is written: "What no eye has seen, what no ear has heard, and what no human mind has conceived"— the things God has prepared for those who love him—
1 Corinthians 2:9 NIV

It's essential that we don't take a limited idea of how God intends us to enjoy the world, people, and Him. God gives in abundance and to overflow. God's signature is "more than enough," which you can observe through the Bible and human history. One of the greatest moments in history is recorded in the Bible during the feeding of the five thousand found in the Gospels. After Jesus blessed the little fish and bread the young boy had, he had the disciples distribute it to the crowd, and a supernatural multiplication of heaven took place.

They all ate and were satisfied, and the disciples picked up twelve basketfuls of broken pieces that were left over.
Matthew 14:20 NIV

If God were a "just enough" kind of God, then Jesus would not have multiplied the fish and loaves to have twelve baskets left over; it would have been just enough. But Jesus allows us to see his over-the-top nature to provide and bless in abundance. If we don't embrace the fundamental principles that *God loves us,* desires to *give us good things,* and wants to *bless us in abundance*, we'll never be able to create wealth and overflow in our lives.

Much of our lives flow from how we see. It's how we see ourselves, others, and, most importantly, how we see God. If we see God as stingy and withholding, we'll receive from Him in that way. Often, Jesus would tell people that they received it according to their faith (how they see and believe). Do you see yourself as a favored child of God who has been placed right in the middle of all God's best? Or do you see yourself as always trying to earn his love and not worthy of abundance and enjoyment? This was a part of what I had to get a greater revelation on. I had to move from believing God was reluctantly taking care of me to seeing God as an excited father planning to do good things for his children. He longs to show you His goodness and abundance. He created so much enjoyment in the world that isn't technically essential for living but purely for beauty and fulfillment.

And like a good father, while I want to give my children the best of all creation, I also know that sometimes the things they want aren't always what's best for them. So, there may be times when God stops or holds back something we want because He sees the bigger picture and knows what's best for us. We can trust and rely on the heart of God and his desire to bless us; we can also trust God knows better than we do, and when something that we desire seems to be withheld, we can trust that God is doing that because He loves us as well.

I will give thanks and praise to You, for I am fearfully and wonderfully made; Wonderful are Your works, And my soul knows it very well. My frame was not hidden from You, When I was being formed in

secret, And intricately and skillfully formed [as if embroidered with many colors] in the depths of the earth. Your eyes have seen my unformed substance; And in Your book were all written The days that were appointed for me, When as yet there was not one of them [even taking shape]. How precious also are Your thoughts to me, O God! How vast is the sum of them!
Psalm 139:14-17 Amplified Bible

Hole In One Favor

This lesson of God's goodness was reinforced on the golf course recently. In a particular round of golf with Pastor Jurgen, Jon Heinrichs, and Peter Snyder, I had an early round par 3 that I missed my drive right, and it hit a tree, and the tree threw the ball right back into the fairway. It's always nice when that happens. As that hole ended, I said, "I'm thankful for the favor, but the Holy Spirit is most likely saying that while he wants to show me favor, it's time for me to play better golf." I was kinda joking, but then Peter Snyder stopped me and said, "Pastor, don't limit God's grace." And it hit me, you're right, "I'll take all the favor and grace from God!" In that round, I had another epic grace-filled bounce out of a tree to the fairway, and then on hole 17, I got my first Hole in one!! I truly believe God was removing another layer of a performance mindset. This book teaches work ethic and good stewardship. But, there's a favor factor that we walk in as His children that is beyond my performance and effort and rests in my heavenly father's desire to give me good things. Let's shift from a begging God to be good to us mindset to expecting God's goodness to flow toward us!

Life to the Full

The thief comes only to steal and kill and destroy; I have come that they may have life, and have it to the full.
John 10:10 NIV

It's vital that we don't see God as an enemy of enjoyment, as if God wants you to live a life that's just barely worth living. Jesus came to give you life and life to the full! God doesn't prioritize your enjoyment to the detriment of your soul and future, but He does want you to be at peace and full of joy. Just like I want for my kids. Let's honor God by taking full advantage of all the beauty and goodness He created for us. On Memorial Day, we often say that the best way to honor the fallen who gave their lives for our freedom is to live fully and completely. Step into all that God has called you to. Don't live small and safe; go after every drop of your purpose!

Don't Worry about Your Life

Then Jesus said to his disciples: "Therefore I tell you, do not worry about your life, what you will eat; or about your body, what you will wear. For life is more than food, and the body more than clothes. Consider the ravens: They do not sow or reap, they have no storeroom or barn; yet God feeds them. And how much more valuable you are than birds! Who of you by worrying can add a single hour to your life? Since you cannot do this very little thing, why do you worry about the rest? "Consider how the wild flowers grow. They do not labor or spin. Yet I tell you, not even Solomon in all his splendor was dressed like one of these. If that is how God clothes the grass of the field, which is

here today, and tomorrow is thrown into the fire, how much more will he clothe you—you of little faith! And do not set your heart on what you will eat or drink; do not worry about it. For the pagan world runs after all such things, and your Father knows that you need them. But seek his kingdom, and these things will be given to you as well. 'Do not be afraid, little flock, for your Father has been pleased to give you the kingdom. Sell your possessions and give to the poor. Provide purses for yourselves that will not wear out, a treasure in heaven that will never fail, where no thief comes near and no moth destroys. For where your treasure is, there your heart will be also.
Luke 12:22-34 NIV

It's easy to get worried about things of lesser importance. Know that your heavenly father knows your needs and is working to provide for you. While we do have to think about and get strategic about the problems we need to solve, we don't have to move into worry and fear because we can and should put our trust in God! Worry is a feeling that flows from the wrong focus. When you find yourself fearing and worrying, stop and ask yourself what is getting the primary attention of your mind? What are you meditating on? Choose to fix your mind and heart on God's Word and His faithful track record. As you focus on His goodness, you'll find anxiety begins to dissipate and hope begins to swell.

Chapter 9

The Contentment Key

But godliness with contentment is great gain. For we brought nothing into the world, and we can take nothing out of it. But if we have food and clothing, we will be content with that. Those who want to get rich fall into temptation and a trap and into many foolish and harmful desires that plunge people into ruin and destruction. For the love of money is a root of all kinds of evil. Some people, eager for money, have wandered from the faith and pierced themselves with many griefs.
1 Timothy 6:6-11 NIV

Better a little with the fear of the Lord than great wealth with turmoil. Better a small serving of vegetables with love than a fattened calf with hatred.
Proverbs 15:16-17 NIV

Contentment is central to Biblical wealth. We must learn to be content where we are on the way to where we're going. Contentment begins with thankfulness. Are you and I living from a place of thankfulness and appreciation for all God has given us? Contentment doesn't mean that you don't have goals and dreams. Instead, it means you don't buy into the lie that you won't be happy, fulfilled, or at peace until you have the "next level" you are dreaming about. Contentment means I find joy and fulfillment in Jesus and all He's given me. It means that I pursue the purposes of God out of joy and obedience, not out of frustration for not having enough yet.

Wealth doesn't Satisfy

Whoever loves pleasure will become poor; whoever loves wine and olive oil will never be rich.
Proverbs 21:17 NIV

Many motivational speakers try to get you dissatisfied with where you're at in a way that motivates you toward greater dreams. There is an element of value in this because you don't want to allow yourself to get comfortable with mediocre living or get comfortable and settle short of the purposes of God. But the lie that you need "more" to be happy is a lie. We need to find contentment and peace right where we're at. The Apostle Paul said, "I've learned to be content in every circumstance." When you talk to people who have been to the metaphorical top of fame or fortune, they will always tell the story of how they assumed it would help satisfy, but it never did. My friend Xola, who formerly went by Kid Sensation, was on the Grammy stage with Sir Mix-a-lot when he won his Grammy. He noted all those smiles were fake. No one is fulfilled or happy. Chasing wealth to satisfy the voids is an endless pit. The overflow of knowing God is a fulfilled life. Chasing and pursuing money, fame, and influence will leave you always needing more.

Delayed Gratification

The wise store up choice food and olive oil, but fools gulp theirs down. Proverbs 21:20 NIV

Wisdom is contentment. Learning to delay instant gratification is central to increasing and multiplying. Delayed gratification is a necessary discipline. Many people are too focused on immediately satisfying their desires rather than patiently building wealth over time. Are you at peace with where God has you, or are you striving and stressed about reaching the next level? Over the years, one of the leading voices on delayed gratification has been Dave Ramsey. I love his iconic quote challenging us to be content and patient now for the greater payoff and enjoyment later. There's no need to try to "keep up with the Joneses." It's a dangerous and sabotaging spirit of this world to be consumed with comparison and envy.

If you will live like no one else now, later, you can live like no one else. Dave Ramsey

Does envy have you drained of joy and thankfulness?

A heart at peace gives life to the body, but envy rots the bones. Proverbs 14:30 NIV

A faithful person will be richly blessed, but one eager to get rich will not go unpunished. To show partiality is not good— yet a person will do wrong for a piece of bread. The stingy are eager to get rich and are

unaware that poverty awaits them. Whoever rebukes a person will in the end gain favor rather than one who has a flattering tongue. Whoever robs their father or mother and says, "It's not wrong," is partner to one who destroys. The greedy stir up conflict, but those who trust in the Lord will prosper.
Proverbs 28:20-25 NIV

Faithfulness produces wealth, but being overly focused on wealth will punish you with an unhealthy life. One of the things that causes poverty and drains our happiness is when we look around and wish we had what others have. It can pull us out of appreciation and into envy and greed. It's a matter of trusting God. Do you believe that God knows how to give you good things or not? Envy causes us to rush quickly to instant satisfaction of wants, usually to the detriment of ourselves and our financial picture.

If someone asks me about making more money, I ask them "why" before I tell them "how."
Dario Deluca
Real Estate Developer

Seasons and Promises

So Joshua said to the Israelites: "How long will you wait before you begin to take possession of the land that the Lord, the God of your ancestors, has given you?
Joshua 18:3 NIV

Joshua challenges them to fully take possession of what God has promised them. This is still God's call to all of us: Do not stop short of what God has for you. Contentment doesn't mean settling short of God's promises. Fighting for your purpose and God's promises is different from stepping into coveting something that isn't yours or isn't your season yet. We need to understand there's a difference between what has been promised and the season of receiving that promise. We can get ourselves in trouble and frustrated when we assume we should have a harvest from seeds we either haven't planted yet or that we just planted. Yes, you planted, and it's true you have a future promised harvest, but you have to be patient. Similar to other areas of promise, goals, business, dreams, and wealth creation, we have to be patient with the process of the harvest. It's also important to be content with what you've been promised. We think we can have what others have been promised yet fall short because God equipped us for different purposes than others. This causes frustration, pain, and disillusionment. If you're a one-talent guy, don't be frustrated that you're not a 10-talent guy; just put to work what you've been given and grow and expand what God has given you. Most of my frustrated seasons were from trying to get something to produce that I wasn't equipped for. The more I rest in my calling and identity, the more I've enjoyed life and the more fruitful my life has become in all ways of life.

Don't Harvest to the Edge

When you reap the harvest of your land, do not reap to the very edges of your field or gather the gleanings of your harvest. Leave them for the poor and for the foreigner residing among you. I am the Lord your

God.
Leviticus 23:22 NIV

While God wants you to experience the blessing and abundance of His prosperity, there will always be those who, for various reasons, are in a temporary or prolonged season of poverty. As those who have a field and the means to harvest that field, we're called on by God to leave some of the edges of the field un-harvested as a way of being kind to the poor and needy. God wants to bless your life, but as you experience His blessing, God calls on us not to forget others who are struggling. Notice that it doesn't tell them to harvest all of the fields and then give a percentage to the poor; it says to leave a percentage for them to go and get it themselves. The reason here is that God doesn't do handouts to people; he helps us up and gives us the power to create wealth, not to get wealth for free. In our cities, we must work to create opportunities for the needy to work; we shouldn't just be giving handouts to the poor; that temporary fix doesn't serve anyone but the wealthy person's ego. Business owners must look for ways to provide space for those in a tough spot to work and provide for their families. The beautiful thing about increasing and prospering is that the "edges" get bigger, so you can be increasingly generous to those in need. But if we don't live in a place of contentment and always need "more," it will hinder our ability to care for others and showcase the goodness of God to those in need.

Chapter 10

Blessed to be a Blessing

Wealth and prosperity are good for enjoyment, but they aren't the source of it. If we pursue wealth as the source of fulfillment, it will leave us busted and empty. One of the main ways we use the wealth that God brings us is to be a blessing and add value to others. One of the highest purposes of money is to serve, and we should put it to work in that way often. Jesus gives us insight into the power of giving.

In everything I did, I showed you that by this kind of hard work we must help the weak, remembering the words the Lord Jesus himself said: 'It is more blessed to give than to receive.'
Acts 20:35 NIV

It's more blessed to give! That's a powerful statement and truth. Jesus is teaching us how to increase our level of blessing. What we receive when we give is more valuable than what we get from spending that money. It's greater in both the natural and supernatural treasures in heaven. Let's learn to stir up a heart of giving. Let's be known for what we give more than what we have. In a conversation with my pastor, he reminded me that one of the reasons Jesus says this is because receiving is the end of something, and giving is what begins that cycle of giving and receiving. Stay in the flow of God's blessing by staying continuously in a place of giving. This truth is also easily felt in everyday experiences; when we give, it just feels better. God designed us to get a rush of positive emotions when we help and serve others; it's called the helpers high. Your life is better when you serve others, and you feel better when you give and serve.

We make a living by what we get, but we make a life by what we give.
Winston Churchill

Defining Biblical Wealth

What good will it be for someone to gain the whole world, yet forfeit their soul? Or what can anyone give in exchange for their soul?
Matthew 16:26 NIV

The Bible says that God gives us the power or enables us to create wealth. What or how does the Bible define wealth? Is there a different view of being rich from a Biblical perspective to a secular one? The answer is yes and no. On one hand, there's no difference because there's no secular wealth or Christian wealth; there's just wealth. How we view it, make it, or use it is what God's Word governs. Yes, the Bible speaks to being spiritually rich or spiritually poor, but right from the beginning, you see that God speaks about material wealth when, at the beginning, He says he put gold in the ground for us to pull out and put to work.

Wealth itself may not be spiritual, but how we handle our money is impacted by our Spiritual health. Are you leading money or serving it? We have to reject the idea that money or wealth is wrong. It's more about the purpose we give it, or more specifically, knowing the purpose that God has given it. If you are worshiping money, you'll be a slave and be beaten down by it. You'll stay in a state of striving and struggle. But, when you're focused on finding fulfillment in Jesus, you'll keep wealth in its proper place. As the scripture above reminds us, we'll end up poor if we lose ourselves and the things that matter in the pursuit of gaining all the things the world values. The wealthiest man to live was King Solomon, and he said that wisdom is more valuable than gold. He doesn't say that money is worthless, but he reminds us that what ultimately matters and satisfies us are spiritual things. If you have them on a scale, wisdom, peace, passion, love, and forgiveness weigh more than material things.

To define wealth specifically. Being wealthy spiritually means having a relationship with God through the salvation Jesus purchased on the cross. Without that, we are poor, blind, and pitiful. Being naturally wealthy is subjective and different in different nations and eras. Is there a certain level we should achieve, or is there an amount of prosperity that God wants each of his kids to have? No, that's where he leaves it up to us to go and create wealth as we need and desire. The only level we see in the word about wealth is that it's clear God wants us to live in overflow so that we can care for others as needed. For our family, we have lofty goals of impact and enjoyment, but our baseline goal is to build our income streams (working, investments, and passive) to a place where our passive income meets all our expenses with overflow to be a blessing to those around us.

The ark of God remained with the family of Obed-Edom in his house for three months, and the Lord blessed his household and everything he had.
1 Chronicles 13:14 NIV

Too Poor to Be a Christian

We all love reading the heroic story of the good Samaritan that Jesus tells in the book of Luke. A man has been robbed, beaten, and left for dead; the Samaritan comes along and saves the day and cares for all his needs. The story culminates in these two verses.

He went to him and bandaged his wounds, pouring on oil and wine. Then he put the man on his own donkey, brought him to an inn and took care of him. The next day he took out two denarii and gave them to the innkeeper. 'Look after him,' he said, 'and when I return, I will reimburse you for any extra expense you may have.'
Luke 10:34-35 NIV

This is a beautiful story, but the real question is, how many of us have the ability to live out this story that Jesus tells? I heard Craig Groeschel say that most Christians are "too poor to be a Christian." And he was referencing this story. Do we live in a way that we're ready and able to be generous and kind to others when needed and when God calls on us to do something? God's will is that we have the ability to be generous on every occasion.

Now he who supplies seed to the sower and bread for food will also

supply and increase your store of seed and will enlarge the harvest of your righteousness. You will be enriched in every way so that you can be generous on every occasion, and through us your generosity will result in thanksgiving to God.
2 Corinthians 9:10-11 NIV

While God desires to bless you and provide for your enjoyment, having more stuff is not a fulfilling goal. The goal is to enjoy and serve God and people; the goal is to push back the work of the enemy and establish His Kingdom. If you live this way, you'll walk in His blessing. On the other hand, if you chase blessing and personal pleasure without purpose, you'll end up bankrupt in the natural and spiritual.

Whoever shuts their ears to the cry of the poor will also cry out and not be answered.
Proverbs 21:13 NIV

Overflow

Beloved, I pray that in every way you may succeed and prosper and be in good health [physically], just as [I know] your soul prospers [spiritually].
3 John 2 Amplified Bible

God's priority of blessing is inside out; it's soul first and then physical. It's not only that it's the soul first, but the physical is the overflow of the spiritual, which is why the first focus is always on prosperity in your soul. In all ways, naturally and spiritually, my goal is to live in flow and overflow to be able to bless others in addition to taking care of my own family. As a pastor and preacher, my focus is to preach and minister to the heart, mind, and soul of a person because I know that everything flows out of that place. If the soul is wounded and contaminated, it won't be able to produce life and prosperity. Soul health begins at Salvation. By this point in the book, you've seen how God desires to bless those who are His, but he doesn't force us to choose Him. But, all of us, because we're born into sin and an evil world, need to be rescued and brought to life; we need someone to cover our sin. Thankfully, God provided a way through Jesus' death on the cross and resurrection three days later! The Bible says that if you believe this in your heart and confess that Jesus is Lord, you will be saved! You will be brought from death to life! Your soul will be healed and begin to prosper. If today is the day you're making Jesus your Lord for the first time, please reach out to us and let us know; we'd love to send you a gift to help in your next steps with Following Jesus.

Chapter 11

Think Generational

Houses and wealth are inherited from parents,
but a prudent wife is from the Lord.
Proverbs 19:14 NIV

Now I am ready to visit you for the third time, and I will not be a burden to you, because what I want is not your possessions but you. After all, children should not have to save up for their parents, but parents for their children.
2 Corinthians 12:14 NIV

Are you thinking beyond your lifetime with your wealth? Are you thinking about building generational prosperity? Biblical prosperity calls us to think beyond our lifetime; don't let your goals end with you. Think and plan for your kids and your children's children. The Jewish people have embraced this Biblical principle and see a large portion of the world's wealth in the hands of their descendants. A theme in the Bible is to leave an inheritance for your children and grandchildren; we do this spiritually and physically. The most important thing a couple can leave their kids is an example of a personal and passionate relationship with God. But, it's also blessed and Godly for parents to leave a rich legacy of financial blessing to their children and grandchildren. Keeping a generational focus will keep you freer from the momentary entanglements that wealth can bring. Begin teaching and transferring wealth creation principles to your children right now. Don't be quiet about how you build and how you give. Teach your children the Biblical principles found in the Bible that we're highlighting in this book. When possible, partner with them to invest, while they are young, in savings and investments that will set them up at a greater level than even you had. My wife and I talk openly with our kids about giving, investing, and creating wealth. We also have savings and investing accounts that we invest into for our kids and their future. But we don't give them money without them learning to earn and grow their income. Being generationally minded doesn't mean giving our kids free handouts as much as it means teaching, training, equipping them, and empowering them to build on what you've given them. What are you transferring to the next generation? Think both earthly and heavenly.

Do not be overawed when others grow rich, when the splendor of their houses increases; for they will take nothing with them when they die, their splendor will not descend with them.
Psalms 49:16-17 NIV

A Generous Inheritance

A good person leaves an inheritance for their children's children, but a sinner's wealth is stored up for the righteous.
Proverbs 13:22 NIV

We don't need to have the mindset, "I earned it the hard way, and so should you." While we don't give wealth to our kids without them building and growing through the principles, we also don't withhold good things from them. We love our kids and should do everything possible to set them up for success. We want them to feel the generosity of their natural parents in the same way we feel that generosity from our heavenly Father. Everything we do as parents is designed to showcase the nature of God. We're to introduce our children to God's character by the environment we create at home. They'll know God is love by first seeing that Dad and Mom love them, and their know God is generous by seeing that spirit in us as parents.

Also, notice in the above verse, the wealth of the wicked isn't stored up like some heavenly welfare redistribution for Christians. In the parable of the talents, the wealth of the wicked was given to the faithful producer. Our goal as parents is to prepare our children to be faithful and fruitful with what God has given them. That will position them to be the recipients of that store of wealth.

Chapter 12

Establish The Kingdom

David said, "My son Solomon is young and inexperienced, and the house to be built for the Lord should be of great magnificence and fame and splendor in the sight of all the nations. Therefore I will make preparations for it." So David made extensive preparations before his death.
I have taken great pains to provide for the temple of the Lord a hundred thousand talents of gold, a million talents of silver, quantities of bronze and iron too great to be weighed, and wood and stone. And you may add to them.
1 Chronicles 22:5, 14 NIV

Our wealth's central focus should be amplifying the Gospel and establishing the Kingdom of God on earth! We see a great example with King David; he saw the importance of personally investing in the House of God. It's a priority issue and a worship issue. If you're offended at being asked to invest in the house of God but have no problem investing in your home and vacations, then we have an honor and priorities problem. It's worth reading through the whole book of Haggai. It's a powerful picture of how

God wants us to see wealth and how to prioritize the house of God.

In the second year of King Darius, on the first day of the sixth month, the word of the Lord came through the prophet Haggai to Zerubbabel son of Shealtiel, governor of Judah, and to Joshua son of Jozadak, the high priest: This is what the Lord Almighty says: "These people say, 'The time has not yet come to rebuild the Lord's house.'" Then the word of the Lord came through the prophet Haggai: "Is it a time for you yourselves to be living in your paneled houses, while this house remains a ruin?" Now this is what the Lord Almighty says: "Give careful thought to your ways. You have planted much, but harvested little. You eat, but never have enough. You drink, but never have your fill. You put on clothes, but are not warm. You earn wages, only to put them in a purse with holes in it." This is what the Lord Almighty says: "Give careful thought to your ways. Go up into the mountains and bring down timber and build my house, so that I may take pleasure in it and be honored," says the Lord. "You expected much, but see, it turned out to be little. What you brought home, I blew away. Why?" declares the Lord Almighty. "Because of my house, which remains a ruin, while each of you is busy with your own house. Therefore, because of you the heavens have withheld their dew and the earth its crops.
Haggai 1:1-10 NIV

God doesn't say that their paneled (fancy) houses were wrong; it's that there was an honor and priority issue. It highlights why we often find ourselves spinning our wheels in business: because we've made God's purpose secondary. We're invited into the blessing and flow of heaven when we embrace the Kingdom principle of honor. Look over your giving, especially your giving above your tithe. Are you generous towards God's house? Are you sacrificing to see the Gospel expand? Are you building God's House or just consumed with your house?

See, I set before you today life and prosperity, death and destruction. For I command you today to love the Lord your God, to walk in obedience to him, and to keep his commands, decrees and laws; then you will live and increase, and the Lord your God will bless you in the land you are entering to possess. But if your heart turns away and you are not obedient, and if you are drawn away to bow down to other gods and worship them, I declare to you this day that you will certainly be destroyed. You will not live long in the land you are crossing the Jordan to enter and possess.
Deuteronomy 30:15-18 NIV

When you seek the Kingdom of God and follow God's ways, you'll find God's blessing surrounding every step you take. It might take some shifting and adjusting, but take a step back to review the focus of your resources to be sure you have the right priority.

But who am I, and who are my people, that we should be able to give as generously as this? Everything comes from you, and we have given you only what comes from your hand. We are foreigners and strangers in your sight, as were all our ancestors. Our days on earth are like a shadow, without hope. Lord our God, all this abundance that we have provided for building you a temple for your Holy Name comes from your hand, and all of it belongs to you.
1 Chronicles 29:14-16 NIV

SECTION 3

Biblical Wealth Creation Principles

But remember the Lord your God, for it is he who gives you the ability to produce wealth, and so confirms his covenant, which he swore to your ancestors, as it is today.
Deuteronomy 8:18 NIV

The Bible is the complete revelation of who our God is and His plan for humanity's salvation and ultimate redemption. But the Bible isn't just a plan for how to get to heaven through faith in Jesus; it's also packed full of life principles, including great detail on the creation and handling of wealth. In fact, there are well over 2,000 verses in the Bible speaking about wealth, prosperity, income, spending, greed, generosity, employees, caring for the poor, saving, and investing. Deuteronomy 8:18 is a guiding verse for this book. For the rest of this book, we'll uncover Biblical strategies for creating, building, and stewarding wealth.

Scan to watch our

Wealth Creation Interviews:

Chapter 13

Sabbath Principles

Remember the Sabbath day by keeping it holy. Six days you shall labor and do all your work, but the seventh day is a sabbath to the Lord your God. On it you shall not do any work, neither you, nor your son or daughter, nor your male or female servant, nor your animals, nor any foreigner residing in your towns. For in six days the Lord made the heavens and the earth, the sea, and all that is in them, but he rested on the seventh day. Therefore the Lord blessed the Sabbath day and made it holy.
Exodus 20:8-11 NIV

There are two sides to the principle of the Sabbath. The first is trust and honor. God calls us to set time aside weekly to worship and firmly put our trust in Him. The other part of a sabbath is physical recharging and rejuvenation. Rest is truly productive and essential to disconnecting you from the hustle success culture and connecting you to the heart and power of God. The world constantly tries to pull us into stress and fear, but taking time weekly to pause, reflect, worship, and get our eyes on Jesus will breathe life, peace, wisdom, and courage into our souls! When we ignore the Sabbath, we're attempting to make life happen in our own strength and without God's help. If our current financial strategy requires us to grind 24/7, we're doing something wrong. Each nation will have different principles guiding its economic systems that will impact your ability to work and create. The need for a free society is one of the reasons to preach the Gospel; it brings the Biblical moral code that is the greatest liberator of the free market. But within the context of your nation, we must embrace the Sabbath. The Bible shows us that the Jewish nation honored the Sabbath and all Biblical laws in all seasons of prosperity or captivity.

The Sabbath Serves You

Jesus also says that the Sabbath was made for man and not man for the Sabbath, which means we don't need to be religious about it, but we do need to understand that it was created for our health. Honoring the Sabbath also allows for better vision. It provides a space for us to pause, step back, and see our life and work with fresh eyes. Too many get stuck because they grind week in and week out without taking the time to pray, reflect, rest, and recharge. It's incredible how a "stepping-back" moment can help you advance. Even in golf, when I'm on the range, and someone is coaching me, I'll get in a rut, swinging over and over a few times, and then the coach will say, "Why don't you take a step back, shake it off, refocus on your target, and try again." It's a powerful reset, and my next swing will always be better after I've paused and refocused. There may need to be creative ways to do this with the uniqueness of your schedule, but work to prioritize rest. Sunday is most often our day of spiritual restoration and connection as we gather with other believers to worship, and Sunday can also be a great day to take your physical sabbath rest, but you don't need to feel like it has to be. Choose a rhythm of rest that works for you and your family.

Learning to Trust God

The Lord said to Moses at Mount Sinai, "Speak to the Israelites and say to them: 'When you enter the land I am going to give you, the land itself must observe a sabbath to the Lord. For six years sow your fields, and for six years prune your vineyards and gather their crops. But in the seventh year the land is to have a year of sabbath rest, a sabbath to the Lord. Do not sow your fields or prune your vineyards. Do not reap what grows of itself or harvest the grapes of your untended vines. The land is to have a year of rest.
Leviticus 25:1-5 NIV

God didn't just tell the people to take a weekly day of rest; He also had them take a year off of planting a field to let it rest and replenish the ground. This reminds us that there may be seasons when the field we're working in isn't producing, or we need to lay it down. It also reminds us to trust God even when we may not understand the timing. Because I'm sure many families were like, "It's a perfect field; why would we not plant." When we lean into the holy spirit, receive direction, and respond to it, we'll find the work is more fruitful. Our culture is going to focus more on soaking every ounce of profit out of a venture and when it's done move on, but God is thinking more long-term health which requires more rhythms. Leviticus 26 shows how obedience to the Sabbath rest season on the field will produce more abundant fruit than before. When we rest, pause, and worship God, our lives and work are more fruitful and fulfilling. Again, this is a direct challenge and balance to the rushed hustle culture. Instead of trying to force and strong-arm everything, we learn to pull back, reflect, worship, and trust God.

Do not wear yourself out to get rich; do not trust your own cleverness. Cast but a glance at riches, and they are gone, for they will surely sprout wings and fly off to the sky like an eagle.
Proverbs 23:4-5 NIV

Many people wear themselves out chasing more, more, more. Do we trust God, or are we pushing, striving, and stressing ourselves out chasing a certain status? You'll know if you're *trusting* God or *striving* based on how worn out you feel.

Never Retire

Now when David had served God's purpose in his own generation, he fell asleep; he was buried with his ancestors and his body decayed.
Acts 13:36 NIV

On the opposite end of the hustle culture is the fixation on retirement, which is the idea that the goal of life is to get to a time in life where you stop working and just relax until you die. However, retirement isn't a Biblical concept. It's dangerous and deadly to your health and isn't God's intention. So much of culture now jokes about and genuinely works towards this euphoric idea of "not working." Because we've bought into a lie that work is bad, and we'd be happier if we just sipped Mai Tai's on the beach! Now, that's good for a sabbath and a vacation, but when you lay down your mission and purpose that drives you, you begin to die inside, and often, that leads to actual death. Often, couples die within a few years after retirement, not from age but from the death of their purpose and drive. Notice when the Bible instructs the shifting of job responsibility as a priest ages.

This is what applies to the Levites: from twenty-five years old and upward they shall enter to perform service in the work of the Tent of Meeting, but at the age of fifty years, they shall retire from the service of the [tabernacle] work and serve no longer. They may assist their brothers in the Tent of Meeting to keep an obligation, but they shall do no [heavy or difficult] work. Thus you shall deal with the Levites concerning their obligations."
Numbers 8:24-26 Amplified Bible

Priests were instructed to shift their careers from doing the heavy lifting to coaching the younger Levites. What a powerful way to keep mentorship and discipleship growing and building for generations. If you've been called to a specific career or ministry, it may change a bit as you get older; you may shift to helping others at a greater level over doing the work. Remember, Your purpose is God-given, and Your Work is blessed by God.

Work is good and good for you.

Chapter 14

Tithes & Offerings

But seek first his kingdom a nd his righteousness,
and all these things will be given to you as well.
Matthew 6:33 NIV

First things first. Everything works better and flows when we're in the right order. In Chiropractic, the first bone at the base of your scull that the rest of your spine is connected to is called the atlas. If that's off, the rest of the back will be off, and nerves will be pinched, so my Chiropractor (Dr. Matt) begins by setting the atlas first. When we get *first* principles right, we'll see that many of God's principles and promises flow more naturally from this. The starting point of engaging in God's Biblical principles of wealth is through bringing our tithes and offerings. It doesn't mean that all of your financial challenges are due to not tithing because there are other areas of stewardship, as discussed in this book, but tithing is the starting point. Tithing brings us into the flow of God's financial economy. It sets the foundation on which we can build the rest of the Biblical stewardship principles.

Tithing

Honor the Lord with your wealth, with the firstfruits of all your crops; then your barns will be filled to overflowing, and your vats will brim over with new wine.
Proverbs 3:9-10 NIV

Overflow is a response to honoring God with your wealth; with the first! If you want to operate in the flow of God's favor, you need to bring him the whole tithe. What is the tithe? The word tithe means a tenth. It's 10% of ALL that you make. There are few areas of our lives where the Bible uses as strong of language as around the tithe, which we see in these verses in the book of Malachi:

Will a mere mortal rob God? Yet you rob me. 'But you ask, 'How are we robbing you?' 'In tithes and offerings. You are under a curse—your whole nation—because you are robbing me. Bring the whole tithe into the storehouse, that there may be food in my house. Test me in this," says the Lord Almighty, "and see if I will not throw open the floodgates of heaven and pour out so much blessing that there will not be room enough to store it. I will prevent pests from devouring your crops, and the vines in your fields will not drop their fruit before it is ripe," says the Lord Almighty. 'Then all the nations will call you blessed, for yours will be a delightful land," says the Lord Almighty.
Malachi 3:8-12 NIV

Many don't experience the favor of God in their finances because they either rob God by giving nothing or they take a "tipping" approach to their giving rather than a "tithing" approach. God calls for 10%, not 2% or 4% or even 9%, but the whole tithe. Imagine if a married man said he was 90% faithful to his wife. You wouldn't applaud or approve of that because even 99% faithful to your marriage is still 100% unfaithful to your marriage. Bringing any less than 10% is 100% unfaithful with the tithe. If you've created a life that spends to the edge of what you make, it's vital that you quickly adjust your spending or sell what you must to free up the 10%. It's also key that you step out in faith and begin to bring the 10% before you get it all figured out. I love this statement by Pastor Jurgen about tithing:

Everyone who tithes can afford to,
but everyone who doesn't tithe can't afford to.
Pastor Jurgen Matthesius

The truth he's bringing up is that you can't afford it because you are out of alignment. When you get back into alignment with God's Word, you'll see an unlocked flow of favor on your work. Don't hold anything back. Honor God with the first and best.

Woe to you, teachers of the law and Pharisees, you hypocrites! You give a tenth of your spices—mint, dill and cumin. But you have neglected the more important matters of the law—justice, mercy and faithfulness. You should have practiced the latter, without neglecting the former.
Matthew 23:23 NIV

Jesus affirms the importance of bringing your tithe while highlighting the more important matters of justice and mercy. In the topic of tithing, the truth is there are much more important matters. Actually, one of the reasons why tithing is so important to God is less about the money and more about what that money is attached to. While the tithe is functionally used to facilitate certain functions of the Kingdom of God, Jesus isn't a poor bagger coming to his churches asking for a handout, actually, the tithe is one of the pathways to our hearts. The Bible says:

For where your treasure is, there your heart will be also.
Matthew 6:21 NIV

Our heart is linked to our wealth; if we withhold our tithe from God, it's withholding our heart. There's so much blessing released around the tithe because it's God's exchange when we surrender and bring our hearts and our worship to him through our obedient bringing of the tithe. Tithing is worship, it's honor, and it keeps our heart close to God and His purpose.

If you have a challenge with tithing, you don't have a problem with giving; you have a problem with God.
Pat Mesiti
Executive Coach, Author, Pastor

The next passage reinforces the revelation that God is most concerned with having your heart. It also shows some of the operational functions of the tithe.

Be sure to set aside a tenth of all that your fields produce each year. Eat the tithe of your grain, new wine and olive oil, and the firstborn of your herds and flocks in the presence of the Lord your God at the place he will choose as a dwelling for his Name, so that you may learn to revere the Lord your God always. But if that place is too distant and you have been blessed by the Lord your God and cannot carry your tithe (because the place where the Lord will choose to put his Name is so far away), then exchange your tithe for silver, and take the silver with you and go to the place the Lord your God will choose. Use the silver to buy whatever you like: cattle, sheep, wine or other fermented drink, or anything you wish. Then you and your household shall eat

there in the presence of the Lord your God and rejoice. And do not neglect the Levites living in your towns, for they have no allotment or inheritance of their own. At the end of every three years, bring all the tithes of that year's produce and store it in your towns, so that the Levites (who have no allotment or inheritance of their own) and the foreigners, the fatherless and the widows who live in your towns may come and eat and be satisfied, and so that the Lord your God may bless you in all the work of your hands.
Deuteronomy 14:22-29 NIV

Open Heaven

Are you living under an open heaven? In Malachi, it says that when we bring the whole tithe to the house of God (Church), God will open the windows of heaven and pour out so much blessing we won't even be able to contain them. I love how a pastor friend of mine, Eddie Windsor, taught this. Every time we tithe, God opens the windows of heaven. So, if we're tithing but still operating in lack, part of the issue is learning to increase our capacity to hold more of the blessings he's pouring out on us. I've found that to be profound and true in my life. One part of that for me is in my writing. Years ago, I received a prophetic word from a young man during our weekly men's prayer gathering that said, "Every book is a bucket." This word was saying part of the path towards greater wealth creation and capacity to carry the blessing of heaven was to create more buckets that God could fill. So, even this book is both a tool to help you increase your capacity to receive and a bucket that I'll use to receive the blessing of heaven.

Free Will Offerings

I will sacrifice a freewill offering to you; I will praise your name, Lord, for it is good.
Psalms 54:6 NIV

Tithing is our act of trust and obedience. But we're really not being generous toward God until we give beyond our tithe. It's important to note that we bring our tithe and give our offerings. The tithe belongs to the Lord, and the Bible says that we rob God when we don't bring it, but offerings beyond the tithe are free-will offerings that flow from a heart of thankfulness and worship. You'll notice throughout scripture that the acts of generosity rise like worship to God:

One day at about three in the afternoon he had a vision. He distinctly saw an angel of God, who came to him and said, "Cornelius!" Cornelius stared at him in fear. "What is it, Lord?" he asked. The angel answered, "Your prayers and gifts to the poor have come up as a memorial offering before God.
Acts 10:3-4 NIV

The sacrifice of our financial generosity is seen and honored by God. Most of the time, this category is purely an overflow of giving to serve others, and sometimes, there may be a call to give to build the Kingdom of God in a specific way. We see many of these offerings in the Bible. Most of the time, the tithe was gathered to cover the operations and people side of the church and ministry, but it was the generous offerings given that allowed the temples to be built or repaired.

and said to Moses, "The people are bringing more than enough for doing the work the Lord commanded to be done." Then Moses gave an order and they sent this word throughout the camp: "No man or woman is to make anything else as an offering for the sanctuary." And so the people were restrained from bringing more, because what they already had was more than enough to do all the work.
Exodus 36:5-7 NIV

Beyond your tithe, is there a Kingdom work you can give an offering toward? Is your church building a new building or repairing or planting a new church that you can invest in? A couple of my friends, Mark and Courtney Nelson, are part of our church's Vision Builders group, which invests beyond their tithe in the establishment and building of new Awaken Church locations. He described these generous giving opportunities as a joy and also as a weapon or tool in our arsenal to advance. Not only is it advancing the church, but when we live generously, it also unlocks and breaks open more in our own lives. What a powerful revelation and perspective on generosity.

One person gives freely, yet gains even more; another withholds unduly, but comes to poverty. A generous person will prosper; whoever refreshes others will be refreshed. Proverbs 11:24-25 NIV

Count off seven weeks from the time you begin to put the sickle to the standing grain. Then celebrate the Festival of Weeks to the Lord your God by giving a freewill offering in proportion to the blessings the Lord your God has given you. And rejoice before the Lord your God at the place he will choose as a dwelling for his Name—you, your sons and daughters, your male and female servants, the Levites in your towns, and the foreigners, the fatherless and the widows living among you.
Deuteronomy 16:9-11 NIV

Three times a year all your men must appear before the Lord your God at the place he will choose: at the Festival of Unleavened Bread, the Festival of Weeks and the Festival of Tabernacles. No one should appear before the Lord empty-handed: Each of you must bring a gift in proportion to the way the Lord your God has blessed you.
Deuteronomy 16:16-17 NIV

Offerings are worship

While he was in Bethany, reclining at the table in the home of Simon the Leper, a woman came with an alabaster jar of very expensive perfume, made of pure nard. She broke the jar and poured the perfume on his head. Some of those present were saying indignantly to one another, "Why this waste of perfume? It could have been sold for more than a year's wages and the money given to the poor." And they rebuked her harshly. "Leave her alone," said Jesus. "Why are you bothering her? She has done a beautiful thing to me.
Mark 14:3-6 NIV

The sizable sacrifice the woman with the alabaster jar made to Jesus was more than giving; it was an offering. The offering so moved Jesus that He said everywhere the Gospel is preached, her story would be told. Our offerings are worship. It's worship because it has sacrifice. An offering isn't worship if it doesn't require sacrifice. Judas called her worship-offering a waste. To the onlooker, a generous offering may seem like a waste, but to a true worshiper and to Jesus, a generous offering is a beautiful extension of our worship.

Chapter 15

Stewardship

The Lord answered, 'Who then is the faithful and wise manager, whom the master puts in charge of his servants to give them their food allowance at the proper time? It will be good for that servant whom the master finds doing so when he returns. Truly I tell you, he will put him in charge of all his possessions.
Luke 12:42-44 NIV

Faithful, wise, manager, and steward are words God uses to describe how we should handle what God has entrusted to us. To properly build wealth, we must embrace the Biblical understanding that all we have on earth ultimately belongs to God. We are simply stewarding those possessions while we're here. As a steward, it's not just that we hold onto what God has given us, but it's how well we work the land and grow what we've been entrusted with. It's about how we use what we've been given to serve others. Stewardship is about the care, multiplication, and impact of our God-given resources. Like in the parable of the talents/bags of Gold, we all want to be honored as trustworthy stewards of God's resources.

While Tithing is concerned with You being "Faithful" with 10% of

Your money...True Stewardship in The Kingdom requires You to be faithful with 100% of God's resources!
Pedro Adao

The quote above reminds me of a conversation I had with Dario Deluca, a commercial Real Estate investor and a man and family who know their Kingdom assignment. He said that the only problem with tithing your 10% is that some people then assume that the other 90% is theirs. Speaking to the issue that most don't see themselves as stewards of God's resources, and we then don't see the powerful partnership that God wants to have with us in the multiplication of those resources.

Here are four key areas we must strengthen to grow as Godly, wise stewards of our wealth.

Integrity and Character

The Lord detests differing weights,
and dishonest scales do not please him.
Proverbs 20:23 NIV

The bedrock of stewardship is integrity. To be integrous means that you handle all your resources personally or on behalf of your business or client in a 100% truthful and honest way. No doctoring numbers or data, no hidden fine print in contracts, and blatant lies or extortion. This is bad business in every way, but it's also stepping out of the Biblical bounds that God calls us to operate within; when we dodge God's principles, we'll remove ourselves from the covering and blessing of God.

Whatever you do [whatever your task may be], work from the soul [that is, put in your very best effort], as [something done] for the Lord and not for men, knowing [with all certainty] that it is from the Lord [not from men] that you will receive the inheritance which is your [greatest] reward. It is the Lord Christ whom you [actually] serve.
Colossians 3:23-24 Amplified Bible

When employers were surveyed, "Trust" was one of the top desires when hiring someone. Will they be honest and integrous with the time, resources, and opportunity they've been given? It's also what God is looking for. When we're honest with little, God can trust us with much. Don't take an entitled mindset that feels others owe us so we can take a little cut here or there from either our boss or clients.

Business Integrity

"Don't collect any more than you are required to," he told them.
Luke 3:13 NIV

How are you handling business? Don't extort or try to soak people dry. I know for my books, I could try to make a little more from the different resources that I sell, and while there is the general cost of goods increases, I need to make; overall, my goal is not to collect more than is needed. I don't do myself or anyone else a favor when I try to take too much out of a particular person or field. Know what a reasonable harvest is for your work. There have also been many times where I've refunded customers because I realized they were overcharged for something. They didn't know, and I could have left it and enjoyed a little extra, but integrity will pay off because God sees it, and others will find out and honor your honesty. We all have many opportunities to make small compromises; the Bible calls it having "differing weights." When you're unethical and unfaithful, even what you have will be taken away. If you've found that any area of your life is cheating or stealing in any way, choose to repent to God and all involved and decide to do right. I won't pretend I've never cheated anyone from a time or resources standpoint. Depending on the situation, it can be easy to do, but my conviction is always to repent and make it right. And choose to live by principles and convictions. Just like Zacchaeus, once he encountered Christ, it exposed the lack of integrity, and he instantly said, I'll pay back four times what I stole.

Dishonest money dwindles away, but whoever gathers money little by little makes it grow.
Proverbs 13:11 NIV

When I gain wealth dishonestly, I'll find it slipping through my fingers. God cannot bless your business if you're extorting, manipulating, or mishandling your staff or customers. You may be able to find what seems to be a faster way to wealth, but if it requires lies or small levels of cheating, it will fade as quickly as it came. God cannot allow injustice to go on forever. Reject the spirit of the world that would believe that to be successful; you must sometimes bulldoze over people no matter the cost, feeling like the ends justify the means. How we prosper is seen by God and will be rewarded or stopped accordingly.

A fortune made by a lying tongue is a fleeting vapor and a deadly snare.
Proverbs 21:6 NIV

Faithful and Diligent

The hands of Zerubbabel have laid the foundation of this temple; his hands will also complete it. Then you will know that the Lord Almighty has sent me to you.
Zechariah 4:9 NIV

Being a faithful steward isn't just about saying yes to a calling, work, or mission, but it requires that we finish the mission and increase the resources. Being faithful and diligent in God's economy isn't just "showing up" for work; it means giving yourself to whatever you've been given. It means being fruitful. When the servants were called faithful, it was because they were fruitful. Fruitful means you're producing, growing, multiplying, and serving others. If you're not fruitful, then you're not faithful.

A sluggard's appetite is never filled, but the desires of the diligent are fully satisfied.
Proverbs 13:4 NIV

Faithful and diligent stewards don't just begin; they complete. How you start is less important than how you finish. The Bible says that the completion of a thing is more important than its beginning. See the work through to completion. In the Book of Revelations, Jesus continues to emphasize that the rewards are for those who are faithful to the end. Don't allow the difficulty of the season to stop you from finishing your race!

The end of a matter is better than its beginning, and patience is better than pride.
Ecclesiastes 7:8 NIV

Teamwork and Leadership

Two are better than one, because they have a good return for their labor: If either of them falls down, one can help the other up. But pity anyone who falls and has no one to help them up.
Ecclesiastes 4:9-10 NIV

Effectively stewarding what God has given you is going to require a team. We cannot fulfill our purpose on our own. We're not designed that way; God created the world to work interconnectedly. Learn to trust and rely on others; learn to draw on the strength of others. Sometimes, this may mean that you're on someone else's team, and sometimes, this means that you need to build and lead a team. In both cases, you'll need to learn to be a team player and a leader. Team players are those willing to lay down personal pride or agenda for the greater vision of the company, ministry, or project. Are you able to get along well with others? Do people enjoy having you a part of the project? Learning to be a great value to a team will sow seeds for the day when you'll need to gather, build, and lead a team of your own. Often business gets stalled because we try to accomplish it in a silo. I genuinely believe that everything you need is found in the combination of what God put in you and what He's placed in others.

Delegation is a multi-step process. I do; you watch. I do; you help. You do; I help. You do; I watch.
Jon Soriano
CEO, D2D Sales Coach

Creativity and Commitment

To care for and multiply what we've been given will take lots of creativity and commitment. Many get stuck in their work and purpose due to problems and roadblocks that come their way. What do we do with roadblocks? We have two choices: stop and settle, or we can dig deep and solve the problem. Many are conditioned with the mindset that if it's good or even if it's a God-thing, then it should be easy or flow naturally, but the truth is that all missions and ideas and businesses are going to come up against Giants and roadblocks, but it's in those moments that we have to stay committed beyond convenience to finish the work. We must stop seeing hard work as a bad thing and fight through adversity and setbacks in business. The key is creativity. While we can be creative in the sense of style, design, and all of that, what I'm more speaking about is an internal way of seeing all problems with a pre-determined mindset that, with God's help and all that he has provided me, that we can breakthrough whatever is in front of us. Plato said that necessity is the mother of invention. This is so true; most things weren't invented until there was a problem that needed to be solved.

Indeed, most wealth creation begins with solving someone's problem. I know for me, my best-selling book, Following Jesus, [A discipleship resource for new believers], was born out of meeting a need to effectively disciple new believers. At first, I was planning to make it available as a blog on my website, but then other pastors heard about it and requested I make it into a physical book. That book and its resources have gone on to serve over half a million new believers and counting. It was one thing to identify and feel like we found the answer to the problem; it was another to bring that first book to a completed, published, and distributed state! Once you've creatively solved the problem, now you must see it through to completion. I think of hundreds of thousands of people so far that wouldn't have been served if I quit on that project. There will be roadblocks and setbacks, but commit yourself to the course and watch how God can work over time. Develop a grit that can take down giants. That grit grows when you overcome each new challenge without quitting; no matter how big or small, don't let yourself quit on your commitments.

If you falter in a time of trouble, how small is your strength?
Proverbs 24:10 NIV

Chapter 16

Diligence

Lazy hands make for poverty, but diligent hands bring wealth.
Proverbs 10:4 NIV

Go to the ant, you sluggard; consider its ways and be wise! It has no commander, no overseer or ruler, yet it stores its provisions in summer and gathers its food at harvest. How long will you lie there, you sluggard? When will you get up from your sleep? A little sleep, a little slumber, a little folding of the hands to rest— and poverty will come on you like a thief and scarcity like an armed man.
Proverbs 6:6-11 NIV

Diligence is handling your work in a determined, focused, intentional, and persistent way. This Biblical approach to your work will cause the earth to produce wealth for you. There's no blessing on laziness or careless work. Focused and intentional effort will bring reward. We live in a world that sees work, especially hard work, as something to avoid, But God gives us work. Critical elements of your purpose and health flow from our work. One of the most devaluing things for a man, especially, is to be given handouts rather than given work to do. When we add value through our work, it also brings value to us.

This doesn't mean that I get my complete identity in what I do for a living, but to deny its intended God-design to bring purpose and strength to us would also be selling it short for what it is. It's good for us to work and put our hands to the plow.

The craving of a sluggard will be the death of him, because his hands refuse to work. All day long he craves for more, but the righteous give without sparing.
Proverbs 21:25-26 NIV

The righteous approach to work and wealth creation is completely opposite to the spirit of this world. This scripture above reminds us that the craving of the lazy will actually destroy him. Why is that? For two reasons: first, any craving that is against God will be harmful to us, and second, to desire or crave something endlessly without putting in the work to possess it will cause us to lose heart and break down. Then notice the righteous; it says they GIVE! What a powerful contrast; the sluggard craves or wants, but the righteous give from their overflow. It's also contrasting the connection between wickedness and laziness and the connection between righteousness and prosperity. Diligent people are righteous people, and the hands of the diligent will prosper.

Diligence Produces Little By Little

We build wealth little by little. If you're like me, we want to build wealth quickly, but the Biblical principle is that consistent and diligent stewardship of wealth will cause it to grow. While it can be frustrating to only increase incrementally, it allows you to grow into the capacity to properly handle and multiply what you've been given. Now, there will be times when your business or strategy can surge forward, but if you've been doing the fundamentals, you'll be ready to handle the increase.

A little sleep, a little slumber, a little folding of the hands to rest— and poverty will come on you like a thief and scarcity like an armed man.
Proverbs 6:10-11 NIV

In a world of get-rich-quick ideas, strategies, and schemes, we need to go back to God's word, which teaches us that diligence and good old-fashioned work cause us to prosper. When we're diligent and consistent, we'll see things grow. I know that when it comes to writing, each book I've released hasn't always been a best seller, but each book and resource adds to the overall growth picture. At this stage, my writing carries the primary role in our financial picture, but it took hard work to get each new book and devotional written, and I always had reasons to delay or quit the project. We often look for that magical way to the top, but *the magic you're looking for is in the work you're avoiding.*

Don't be someone who looks for the easy way out of something; look for the right way and the best way, which is often the hard way filled with lots of work, blood, sweat, and tears! Never make life and business decisions based on what is the easiest but on what is the best. There's a reason why they say success is often the road less traveled. In my parenting, pastoring, writing, and leading, the best way is often the route of faithful diligence with the mundane rather than some secret quick fix.

Biblical Business Model

Better to be a nobody and yet have a servant than pretend to be somebody and have no food. The righteous care for the needs of their animals, but the kindest acts of the wicked are cruel. Those who work their land will have abundant food, but those who chase fantasies have no sense. The wicked desire the stronghold of evildoers, but the root of the righteous endures. Evildoers are trapped by their sinful talk, and so the innocent escape trouble. From the fruit of their lips people are filled with good things, and the work of their hands brings them reward. Proverbs 12:9-14 NIV

This incredible passage from Proverbs gives us several key insights into how God expects us to work and how he's designed your work to produce abundance. Allow these principles to guide and govern your wealth creation.

1. Don't focus on the outward perception of wealth but on actual prosperity.
2. Live with kindness.
3. Work the land you have, and you will prosper.
4. Don't chase fantasies but legitimate business ventures and careers.
5. Integrity causes generational wealth.
6. Purity in your dealings provides a way out of trouble.
7. How you speak to others will make a difference in what is produced.
8. God designed work to be rewarded. Money flows toward the diligent.

We must reject an entitled mentality that expects something for no work. The Bible clearly calls us to work hard. Later, verse 27 says:

The lazy do not roast any game, but the diligent feed on the riches of the hunt.
Proverbs 12:27 NIV

It's saying that hunters are eaters. If you don't hunt, you don't eat. The Apostle Paul also tells the new church that if someone in the church community refuses to work, they shouldn't eat.

Work Harder or Change Plans?

How do you know if you need to simply work harder or if something you're doing needs to be changed? That's where you need coaching and mentoring because sometimes, we conclude that my current pain means that something is wrong when, most of the time, it just means we're on the right track and need to keep going. Identify a leader to help you assess the effectiveness and viability of your work. Don't endlessly forge ahead without processing with your mentors, and don't quit without processing.

I went past the field of a sluggard, past the vineyard of someone who has no sense; thorns had come up everywhere, the ground was covered with weeds, and the stone wall was in ruins. I applied my heart to what I observed and learned a lesson from what I saw: A little sleep, a little slumber, a little folding of the hands to rest— and poverty will come on you like a thief and scarcity like an armed man.
Proverbs 24:30-34 NIV

Chapter 17

Serving Others

not looking to your own interests but each of you
to the interests of the others.
Philippians 2:4 NIV

Everything in life works better and makes more sense through the lens of serving. God designed wealth to flow toward those who serve. You'll see your value increase when you serve, give, and find ways to strengthen and add value to others. When you lift others up personally and with your business, you'll increase your value to people and, as a result, increase the level of wealth flowing toward you.

Each of you should use whatever gift you have received to serve others,
as faithful stewards of God's grace in its various forms.
1 Peter 4:10 NIV

Poor people have limited ability to lift others out of poverty. In fact, one of the most significant ways to help someone out of the pit of poverty is to get out of the pit yourself. Don't feel bad about prospering; use your position to lower a rope and pull others up with you. That's a key reason for this book; I was in a financial pit until we learned these Biblical wealth principles that we're now sharing with you. Learning how to prosper is shallow if we don't share it with others.

If either of them falls down, one can help the other up. But pity anyone who falls and has no one to help them up.
Ecclesiastes 4:10 NIV

The world will try to pull you into a pie mentality, meaning there are only so many slices to go around, putting you at odds against others; it's difficult to serve others if they are seen as taking your piece. Rabbi Lapin noted that about Cain and Able at the beginning. When Cain heard that God wasn't pleased with His offering but was pleased with Able, instead of making changes to honor God with his life, he saw the need to eliminate Able. Instead of seeing wealth as a pie, God teaches it as a continually flowing river. This is why cities form: We gather closer to serve each other more effectively with our specific abilities and businesses. Being together or close to others isn't a competition but a compliment. See others as bringing you value rather than as your competition. When we consider how "sir names" originated, they were based on the work you did to serve the greater community—for example, Blacksmith, Baker, Smith, and others. Similarly, as I began to write and create resources, I found that my main niche and way of serving was providing resources within the discipleship space. Instead of wishing I was something else or had a better topic or industry, I recognized that God put His hand on me and equipped me to use this gift at a greater level to serve others. I have over a dozen books published now, most of which are in the specific discipleship space. I do have a few other topics and target audiences, like writing and ministry leadership. I'm always thinking about the primary audiences God has given me to serve. I don't need to try to speak to every topic or group because I'll begin to dilute my impact. The more focused I am, the more effective I can be.

When you focus on adding value rather than getting money, you'll find wealth flows toward you.
Vance Roush
CEO of Overflow, Pastor

Build Another Vision First

The one who guards a fig tree will eat its fruit, and whoever protects their master will be honored.
Proverbs 27:18 NIV

Here's another essential Biblical principle: build and advance someone else's dream, and you'll see your dream fulfilled in the process. Don't feel the need to throw off what feels like the restraints of working for someone else. It may not be your long-term place, but what you will learn in serving, observing, and helping someone else succeed will be valuable. It's also a sowing and reaping principle at play. In the Biblical story of Joseph saving the nation of Egypt, Joseph fulfills his epic dream of everyone bowing down to him while only being second in command. Sometimes, we serve another vision for a season before we step into our own, and sometimes, we fully fulfill our purpose within the context of serving someone else. The reality is you're always serving someone else. You're never truly working for yourself, or you'd be out of work. We're always serving others; this is the way God designed it. Some are arrogant and don't want to submit, so they say they want to work for themselves. However, they quickly realize they now work for the customer or manufacturers. Feeling that I always have to be in charge to get where and what I want can be a trap in today's culture. We're always serving others, whether a boss or a customer. But most of the time, we'll build someone else's vision and find our fulfillment within that reality.

Strategic Partnerships

The Lord God said, "It is not good for the man to be alone. I will make a helper suitable for him."
Genesis 2:18 NIV

In the book *Business Secrets from the Bible*, Rabbi Lapin describes how most elements from the periodic table don't work or serve much value on their own but are immensely valuable when combined. Even the water we drink is a combination of two elements. In construction, they found that steel and concrete are perfectly designed to work together in how they expand and contract to complement each other perfectly. We need each other and are stronger together. God provides the raw materials, and we get the privilege of partnering those materials together to build and create. God doesn't make tables; he made trees, and then we create the table. The Bible describes us as a body with many different parts all working together. We find ourselves within each other. You're not your own man or woman; we are all profoundly connected and must be to find ourselves and fulfill our purpose. You don't achieve your purpose on your own. Your personal life, marriage, parenting, friendships, and business will not reach their full potential without partnering with others.

Our identity is found in community, not isolation.
Rabbi Daniel Lapin
Author & Business Coach

Create a Healthy Home

The strength of your wealth doesn't begin with marketplace partnerships but in the kitchen of your home. How's the family doing? Your marriage is the most important earthly partnership you'll ever form. And if you're not married yet, how are you preparing for your future spouse? If you and your spouse begin the wealth-building journey together but then get to the metaphorical top divorced, it won't be worth it. You may be able to climb faster alone, but you won't get as far and won't enjoy the view when you get there if there's no one to share it with. Too many families get sacrificed on the altar of a dream, business, or even ministry; when the dust settles, you realize you lost. Two celebrities in different areas have come out with documentaries recently. Micheal Jordan, the Basketball legend, and Garth Brooks, the country music icon. In both of their journeys to the top, they created a wake of broken relationships and marriages. Both shed tears about what they lost along the way. Remember what the Bible says:

What good is it for someone to gain the whole world,
yet forfeit their soul?
Mark 8:36 NIV

When talking with my pastors about what they

looked for in a campus pastor at Awaken Church, Pastor Jurgen's first response was, "a healthy and strong marriage." I love that because if the home is strong, the rest of life will flow well from there. Even Warren Buffet said that staying married is one of the secrets to wealth. Are you and your spouse on the same page with the vision and pace you're running at? Are you building a life or just making a living? For those with kids, don't wait for your business to thrive before you prioritize them. My wife and I strongly encourage daily and weekly connecting moments. A few times a week, we take a walk together to connect. We try to do a weekly breakfast together and date nights as often as possible. These practices keep us on the same page and partnering together. A healthy home will cause everything else to rise. Not only will your life increase financially, but the quality and enjoyment of your life will elevate.

Chapter 18

Multiple Streams of Income

Invest in seven ventures, yes, in eight; you do not know what disaster may come upon the land.
Sow your seed in the morning, and at evening let your hands not be idle, for you do not know which will succeed, whether this or that, or whether both will do equally well.
Ecclesiastes 11:2,6 NIV

A Biblical model for creating wealth is developing multiple avenues where you're serving others; this creates multiple streams for money to flow toward you. The above verse shows the value of sowing your seed into different fields because you don't know which crop will grow best this season or the next. Most attempt to prosper purely from one 9-5 paycheck. Some have a great, high-paying, steady job, which is wonderful. Still, I'd encourage you to focus your job's earnings on saving and investing to create other investments that will produce long-term since almost all jobs have a cap to their earning potential. There will be highs and lows in your career that can be a challenge if it's your only source of income.

Multiple Streams of Income could include:

- Your current employment
- Starting your own business
- Investments
- Stock Market
- Creating passive income
- Digital Information Products
- Inventing
- Resource development
- Speaking
- Real Estate
- Training and coaching

One of the primary benefits of multiple income streams is financial freedom. Robert Kiyosaki calls it breaking free from the rat race. Financial freedom comes when our passive income covers and exceeds our living and giving expenses. Passive income is money you make from business, interest, rent, or something similar while you sleep, metaphorically or literally. Maybe it's subscription-based; perhaps it's rental income or investment returns. But make it your goal to build passive income options. For me, writing has become a passive income flow. After the initial investment to write the book, my website, Amazon, and other partnering organizations generate monthly income without additional sales efforts. My wife and I have several streams of income we're developing. We earn interest from our investments, income from Real Estate sales, income from our role as pastors, income from stocks, and passive income from the books we write that serve churches. We also have income from speaking and coaching and other digital information products. We're heavily focused on these current fields God gave us and are always open and looking for more fields where income can be generated as God brings them in our path. However, as our lane of focus has become clearer, I keep my primary attention on these already established streams so that I don't get too diluted in my focus and attention.

Creating a New Stream of Income

Take inventory of your different passions, skills, abilities, and experience. There may be an obvious idea that comes to the surface that you know is available that you haven't executed; perfect, begin there. Some of the ideas may be able to start with your sweat equity, and some may require that you come to the table with investment funds. If more funds are needed, consider what extra side job you can take to set aside the money needed to begin your new venture. Before launching into a new focus, seek wisdom and counsel from a trusted advisor. As the Bible says, plans fail for lack of counsel. This additional time to get advice will save you time and money in the long run.

Once you and/or your spouse identify a new income stream and have sought counsel, take decisive action to step out and begin. As they say, the best time to start saving or investing was 20 years ago; the second best time is right now. If you're adding a side hustle to generate extra income, don't get discouraged by the extra hours and fatigue that it brings. It's a needed investment to break free from the money merry-go-round of just barely paying your bills.

Focus On The Fruit

The ax is already at the root of the trees, and every tree that does not produce good fruit will be cut down and thrown into the fire.
Luke 3:9 NIV

Stop unfruitful ventures. Too many people waste a lot of time and money on ideas and ventures that aren't producing fruit. If there's no fruit, evaluate why. Make adjustments and try again. But, if no fruit is coming, cut down the vine or the tree. Pour gasoline on a fire, and it will expand; throw gasoline on the ground, and it will disappear. If there's no flame, it may be time to move on to more fruitful work. One of the biggest reasons this is a problem is that we often want to be good at something or be known for something completely opposite of our actual gifting. If you're naturally successful in a certain area of life, there's a reason for that: lean into that space.

Chapter 19

Faith & Tenacity

The sluggard says, "There's a lion outside!
I'll be killed in the public square!"
Proverbs 22:13 NIV

Courage is a quality you'll find in all successful people. Making a difference in people's lives and building something valuable will require bold faith and courage. However, few succeed because they are unwilling to take the risks. Taking risks isn't only for increase and growth; it's a foundational principle that God calls us to live beyond our ability and engage in faith with God. Faith activates your full potential. We don't unlock everything in a purely natural sense. We must step out in courage and put our trust in God to release elements of our capacity and calling we cannot access through calculation and passivity. Here's the good news: Courage often builds as you go. One common challenge for people is waiting until they feel fully confident or bold before they take a step. But the truth is that boldness comes to those who move! When God would speak to different leaders in the Bible who were afraid or unsure, He would tell them, "Do not fear!" and remind them that He is with them, and then tell them to go in the strength they have! Moses and Gideon both pushed back with excuses of fear but then became wildly courageous and victorious once they took a step and got going. What decisions have you been avoiding because the conditions aren't perfect? What work have you stopped because "there's a lion in the street?" It's time to take the next step. Often, that first step is taken with fear, still trying to stop you, but take the step, and you'll unlock courage.

Timing

Whoever watches the wind will not plant; whoever looks at the clouds will not reap.
Ecclesiastes 11:4 NIV

Most won't execute because they assume you have to wait for perfect conditions to write the book, start the company, or get the education you need to level up at work, but there will never be a perfect time for most of the things you need to do to succeed. Have you heard the statement, "Done beats perfect." This is a great way to think about making moves. Don't wait until you feel all T's are crossed and "I's" are dotted, or you'll never finish the story. Step out in faith before you feel like you're ready. When you're praying and asking God for the next step, trust God and move as He directs.

Don't Quit

David also said to Solomon his son, "Be strong and courageous, and do the work. Do not be afraid or discouraged, for the Lord God, my God, is with you. He will not fail you or forsake you until all the work

for the service of the temple of the Lord is finished.
1 Chronicles 28:20 NIV

God will see you through to victory if you don't quit. Many won't see their dreams and purposes fulfilled, not because they aren't skilled or resourced enough, but simply because they quit too soon. Where's your tenacity? Where's your grit to stay in the fight until it's done? If you started something, finish it! If you began to build, complete the project. If you got married, see it through "until death do you part." We have an epidemic of quitting, and it creates more pain than the pain of staying in the fight ever could. One of the massive differentiating factors in successful people is their courage, their ability to do what's right in the face of difficulty, uncertainty, danger, and failure. You can hear from God and get a strategy, but ultimately, you must work the plan. You have to begin to take steps and finish what you started.

More Difficult Than You Think

In a previous season of our ministry journey, we served in the northwest, and our pastors, Kevin and Sheila Gerald, and I knew it was time to step out and make a move. This is fun to say initially in a planning or prayer session, but it's another thing to actually uproot your family and go out into the unknown. During that season of praying about what's next in our calling and ministry, God sent a pastor, Mike Unversagat, with a prophetic word to connect with me during one of our conferences. He said, without knowing what we were praying about, that in this next season, we'd have an easier choice and a difficult choice and that we should choose the more difficult one, which was to go down to San Diego, where we had no job and no guarantees. Then he stopped me and said, "Now, you need to know, it's going to be harder than you think." That may not sound encouraging, but it became a great source of encouragement in those beginning seasons in San Diego when we almost didn't make it. Part of why I could keep fighting through was because I knew God had already warned me of the difficulty we would face.

In those difficult seasons, the things that carried me through were:

1. Consistent time in worship and God's presence
2. Daily time in the Bible
3. An incredible wife to believe and partner with
4. Church family to bring encouragement
5. My focus on the prophetic words God had given
6. Knowing a God-dream still requires a fight
7. A commitment to finish the mission God gave me

My advice is to go for it! Activate that dream and passion inside of you! Don't shrink back in fear! Step up and into the assignment. Step out in faith, trust God, and take a step! Courage isn't being completely unafraid; courage is feeling afraid but trusting God and doing it anyway!

Chapter 20

Reputation

A good name is more desirable than great riches;
to be esteemed is better than silver or gold.
Proverbs 22:1 NIV

Do you have a good name? How's your reputation with others? The current culture can devalue the importance of having a good name by saying, "It doesn't matter what anyone else thinks of you." Or that we don't need to "please anyone, just do what you want to do." This isn't wisdom, and unfortunately, it isn't how life works. While it's true that you don't draw your eternal value from the opinions of others, the way others view you is a form of currency. That's why your character and name are so valuable; it's the currency you'll use to build. It's why "word of mouth" marketing is and always will be the best form of marketing. If you take care of people well and treat your family, friends, clients, customers, and business partners with integrity, honor, and hospitality, you'll see your worth and business thrive. When you have a bad reputation as someone who doesn't keep his word or always cuts corners, you'll get negative reviews, and people will avoid you and what you offer. My dad, George Deuth, is a man of great integrity in all things and understands the power of a good name. He runs a construction company that does a lot of residential home remodels, which means he's working directly with homeowners. His motto is, "I'm not done until you're happy." He does the job until it's done right, and the customer is happy. He will sometimes adjust and change his work to make the customer happy at his own expense. But because of that, over the years, people around the city began to say if you want it done well, "Let George Do it!" And as you can imagine, it caused him to grow a business that always had more than enough work.

How to create a good name:

1. Do what you say you're going to do
2. Deal honestly with people
3. Do more than what's expected
4. Care about the person you're serving
5. Be kind and treat people with respect
6. Communicate clearly
7. Admit when you've failed and make it right

Overcoming Failure

for though the righteous fall seven times, they rise again, but the wicked stumble when calamity strikes.
Proverbs 24:16 NIV

You're going to face difficulties and setbacks in your life and, specifically, in your financial journey. Expect challenges rather than being shocked by them when they come. No one becomes prosperous without hard work and without the ability to overcome difficulty when it comes. In fact, many millionaires have gone through several bankruptcies. Why? Because they took risks, failed, and got back up again. In America, we intentionally created the opportunity for bankruptcy to encourage people to pursue their dreams even when it's risky. Because only those who fail forward end up solving problems and serving people. When you have a setback or even a moral failure, the greatest key is to admit it and apologize where needed. When we try to defend ourselves by justifying some of our actions, we keep our reputation in a broken state. Authenticity and taking responsibility for your actions go a long way in restoring your reputation.

Restoring Strength

And David was greatly distressed; for the people spake of stoning him, because the soul of all the people was grieved, every man for his sons and for his daughters: but David encouraged himself in the Lord his God.
1 Samuel 30:6 KJV

While rebuilding your reputation with others, it can be a discouraging season, so you must learn to encourage yourself in the Lord. If you surround yourself with great people, they will be a key source of encouragement, but even if those in your corner are exceptional, there will be times when God teaches you how to get alone with him and learn to draw your strength from Him alone. You have to learn to run to God, encourage yourself, and build yourself up using the Word of God!

Chapter 21

Remember The Poor

James, Cephas and John, those esteemed as pillars, gave me and Barnabas the right hand of fellowship when they recognized the grace given to me. They agreed that we should go to the Gentiles, and they to the circumcised. All they asked was that we should continue to remember the poor, the very thing I had been eager to do all along.
Galatians 2:9-10 NIV

There is a lot to be said about creating wealth, but God also clearly states throughout His word that we are expected to be generous to others as a reflection and response to God's generosity toward us. Prospering allows you to be generous to those in need, and as your business grows, you can provide jobs. What are ways that we can intentionally care for and help the poor? Our desire must be to continue to show compassion toward everyone trapped in any addicted and debased state. I love this scripture:

He who is gracious and lends a hand to the poor lends to the Lord,
And the Lord will repay him for his good deed.
Proverbs 19:17 Amplified Bible

God always sees and responds to those who care for the less fortunate on His behalf. Now, what are the best ways to help the poor? That's a great question, and most of the time, just throwing money at someone bagging for money isn't the best option. Yes, there are times we need to overlook their mistakes and care for someone in need, but in the long term, we want to find ways to encourage, develop, and support them in rising up out of poverty. As a family, we continue to be generous in helping the poor through our giving to our church's missions programs, through the LA Dream Center, and by supporting children overseas through different compassion efforts, as well as finding every opportunity we can to help those in need around us. While there are real reasons people are in poverty, often it might be their fault; we must not move into cynicism and disdain towards them; instead, we extend love and mercy and help them rise.

The generous will themselves be blessed,
for they share their food with the poor.
Proverbs 22:9 NIV

SECTION 4

Wealth Multipliers

One person gives freely, yet gains even more; another withholds unduly, but comes to poverty. A generous person will prosper; whoever refreshes others will be refreshed.
Proverbs 11:24-25 NIV

In this section, we'll get more granular by leaning into key practices and strategies that will help you steward what you have and increase your ability to serve people; in return, you'll see your wealth and impact increase. Many assume financial secrets are being withheld from them, which is why they haven't prospered. This version of a victim mentality leaves us settling for where we are because we assume we'll never get those secrets. Or we assume others have some advantage we don't have that makes us ineligible to succeed. But, the truth is that wealth building and multiplying is the result of applying the fundamentals, so if you're willing to commit to the work, everyone has the ability to prosper. Part of the ability to prosper comes from being in an atmosphere where people are allowed to buy and sell and create value and wealth freely. Some nations facilitate this better than others. If you're reading this in a country that oppresses its people, focus on applying as many of these principles as you're able and equally pray and focus on electing Godly men and women who will usher in greater times of freedom and prosperity based on Biblical principles.

Scan to watch our

Wealth Creation Interviews:

Chapter 22

Vision & Strategy

Where there is no revelation, people cast off restraint; but blessed is the one who heeds wisdom's instruction.
Proverbs 29:18 NIV

Seeing beyond where you are right now is essential to wealth creation. Vision drives and directs you. When God gives vision to us, it's like He is depositing an internal true north compass that keeps guiding us in the right direction. Getting clarity on what you're called to do will help you increase and multiply; it's hard to grow when you're uncertain about your purpose and direction. Implementing a plan to achieve that vision is what separates those who fulfill their purpose from those who don't. If we don't determine our target and create a strategy to get there, we'll stay stuck reacting to the moments life brings us. Sometimes, we get nervous to choose a direction for fear of missing another better opportunity. However, I've learned the power of being decisive. The word decision means to cut away all options but one. Many people fail and falter in life because they fail to choose their vision. Decisions move us forward. If we fail to say yes to the right things and no to the wrong, we'll stall out and never fulfill our purpose.

The Lord said to Abram after Lot had parted from him, 'Look around from where you are, to the north and south, to the east and west. All the land that you see I will give to you and your offspring forever. Genesis 13:14-15 NIV

God says to Abram, I'll give you what you see. There's a principle there. Do you have a vision for what you're stewarding? God has great things in store for us, but we need to be able to see it! We don't just need vision when the business or organization is ours but even when we work for someone else. We need to ask God to give us a greater vision for what's next. Vision is both imparted and discovered. Sometimes, the dream and focus come from within you as a prophetic impartation from God, and sometimes, the vision seems to come from around you from the needs of the world you're living in. Either way, take the time to notice what God is saying and what He is showing you. If something in the world frustrates and angers you, most likely, you've been called to be a part of solving that in the world. If God keeps revealing a dream to you or a passage from the Bible keeps highlighting something, you can be sure that He's leading and calling you into a specific work.

The High Calling is whatever God calls you to.
Colin Higginbottom | CEO, Wealth Creator, Pastor

Wisdom

The plans of the diligent lead to profit as surely as haste leads to poverty.
Proverbs 21:5 NIV

Rushing forward without taking the time to seek wisdom and create a strategy for the vision will lead to poverty. Most of the time, the idea that "I must act on this opportunity now" and have no time for council is a sales tactic and rarely an opportunity that will produce. Haste can lead to bad decisions, and impatience can cause us to quit the opportunity too soon. Stay consistent and determined to see the work through.

The beginning of wisdom is: Get [skillful and godly] wisdom [it is preeminent]! And with all your acquiring, get understanding [actively seek spiritual discernment, mature comprehension, and logical interpretation].
Proverbs 4:7 Amplified Bible

Wisdom is the ability to apply knowledge and insight correctly. Many smart people make dumb decisions. But when we seek Godly wisdom and make the needed decisions to adjust and shift in that direction, we are wise, and it will reward us. Don't reject or ignore wisdom and wise counsel. An important factor in walking in wisdom is humility when taking advice and correction. Sharpen your skills and seek fresh wisdom from Heaven and Earth. Look at this next verse; it says wisdom builds the house.

By wisdom a house is built, and through understanding it is established; through knowledge its rooms are filled with rare and beautiful treasures.
Proverbs 24:3-4 NIV

Strategy

Commit to the Lord whatever you do, and he will establish your plans.
Proverbs 16:3 NIV

The Bible speaks a lot about having a plan. If you're going to fulfill the vision, strategy will be required. Building and advancing financially doesn't happen accidentally; you must make plans. We submit those plans to God for wisdom, guidance, and adjustments, but then we work the plan. The people in the parable of the bags of gold multiplied their resources, which required a plan. The two faithful servants doubled what had been given, which requires wisdom and strategy. If you've been in a plateau season, get input to ensure you don't need a new strategy. Sometimes, those seasons are a normal part of the seasons of life, but make sure you don't stall out continuing with a faulty plan. Get wisdom and make adjustments to the plan. You may have a mission you're called to, which won't change, but a new era may require a new strategy to fulfill the mission.

A key to success is being willing to adjust the business plan as you go.
Anthony Trimino
CEO of Traffik

From a young age, I knew my mission was ministry; that has never changed, but how I fulfilled that mission has adjusted many times. Keep adjusting, evaluating, and implementing new strategies to fulfill your vision. Your ability to see the changes needed further in advance is vital to adjusting and shifting with the seasons. *Plans Change; Vision Remains*

Focus on Net Worth

Wealthy people don't limit their financial vision to paychecks; they think about their collective wealth picture, which is their net worth. Net worth is the total value of your assets minus your liabilities and debts. We initially focused on growing our working income to build wealth in other areas, such as investing and more extensive wealth-creation opportunities.

Our Net Werth builds from:

- Working Income
- Savings
- Investing
- Simplification
- Passive income

Like in the multiple streams of income conversation, approaching your wealth building from a broader and more holistic approach will strengthen and stabilize your vision.

Vision Unfolds

Plans and purpose often unfold as we go. You may not always see the exact steps over the next 10 years, but you can take the next step. You may be afraid to make the wrong choice or to choose the wrong business, but like they say, it's easier to adjust a ship that's already moving than one parked in the harbor. Just as a laser is focused light, your life will increase in impact when you focus and dial in. Don't get trapped by the paralysis of analysis; choose your direction today, Trust God, and take a step. A note: plans can often change while vision remains. Many people get stuck in their business or vision because they hold their plans tighter than their vision. When you do that, it hinders your ability to adjust to the changing market, and it may limit a new business venture that isn't currently in your scope. Boldly step out in the direction of the Vision that God has given you!

Chapter 23

Saving & Debt Payoff

Now he who supplies seed to the sower and bread for food will also supply and increase your store of seed and will enlarge the harvest of your righteousness.
2 Corinthians 9:10 NIV

While we're called to be generous in giving and sowing to establish the Kingdom, we're also given bread for food and seeds to be used to produce and create more. If we're going to increase, one of the greatest secrets is saving to invest in new streams of income. A book I highly recommend is The Richest Man in Babylon. There are tons of simple takeaways to apply immediately. One takeaway is the commitment to give 10% and save 10% from your income for investing. Setting aside the 10% for investing will position you to leap ahead. Why? Because when an investment opportunity comes up, you'll be in a prime position to do something about it. Your investment savings grow quite fast when you commit to them. Be sure to withdraw your tithe and savings immediately.

Joseph said to the people, "Now that I have bought you and your land today for Pharaoh, here is seed for you so you can plant the ground.

But when the crop comes in, give a fifth of it to Pharaoh. The other four-fifths you may keep as seed for the fields and as food for yourselves and your households and your children."
Genesis 47:23-24 NIV

Genesis 47 says that the harvest will be seed for your next crop/planting and that it's food for you to eat. Every harvest is seed and food. Every harvest needs to be used for investment and enjoyment. Don't eat or enjoy all your seed, or you won't have any left to plant and multiply. Likewise, don't plant all your seed and have nothing to eat and enjoy.

Start saving early. Don't wait till you're making a lot of money to save; start now.
Andre Johnson
Coach, Pastor, Investor

Four Savings accounts

Let's chat about savings strategies. Recently we had a beautiful Kingdom focused couple, who thrive both financially and influentially in the marketplace, shared how they fight to live off 50% of their income to accelerate their giving, investing, and income multiplication. That may seem far off for many, but it's a great goal to head towards. T. Harv, who I've referenced in this book, gives his strategy for different savings accounts that help you strastegically prepare your way forward.

- Savings Account
- Emergency Fund
- Investment Account

- Fun/Play Account

Whatever works best for you is fine, but the key is to be intentional about saving for both enjoyment and advancement. We do retirement savings, buffer or emergency savings, and investment savings. We use various accounts for this, but a flexible and high-yield savings account is through (WIF) Wesleyan Investment Financial. It's a great savings account, and even greater is their focus on funding the building of Churches around the World.

Paying Off Debt

As you're applying new wisdom and deploying new habits, it's also important to be patient with yourself in the process. We usually get ourselves stuck in a rut over a long period of time but then want to get out overnight. Just like weight loss. There was a season where I finally reached a point in my weight where I said, "This is enough." I needed to lose 25+ pounds to get back to a healthy spot. Of course, I wish I could have lost all of the weight the next day, but it took four years to get myself there, and it was going to take some time to get out. It was about a four-month journey back to the health I wanted; it was filled with wins and setbacks along the way, but I stayed focused and fought my way out.

Debt Payoff seems really slow at first, but when you stay disciplined at about two-thirds paid off, it just goes quickly. Also, Once I started giving, that's when my debt payoff really began to pay off.
Dr. Kevin Dette
Chiropractor & Coach

Chapter 24

Goal Setting & Budgeting

Whoever can be trusted with very little can also be trusted with much, and whoever is dishonest with very little will also be dishonest with much. So if you have not been trustworthy in handling worldly wealth, who will trust you with true riches? And if you have not been trustworthy with someone else's property, who will give you property of your own? "No one can serve two masters. Either you will hate the one and love the other, or you will be devoted to the one and despise the other. You cannot serve both God and money.
Luke 16:10-13 NIV

Learning to steward and manage our current finances well precedes being able to handle the increase that God wants to bring to the business we're engaged in. Creating goals for your personal and business life and partnering that with a budget is a crucial first step towards multiplication. You can tithe and pray for God's blessing, but if you're being wasteful with your time and money, don't expect favor and increase.

Goal Setting

Too often, trying to accomplish a large vision all at once feels overwhelming. Starting that business, getting out of debt, or even buying a home can feel like a large giant to tackle; this is why we establish goals. Goals are shorter targets to aim at based on the vision and strategy you've already set out. Goals keep us heading in the direction of our vision. Dr. Matt Hubbard has an annual Goal-Setting Seminar that I highly recommend. He teaches powerful strategies for establishing yearly, quarterly, monthly, and weekly goals. People take different approaches to clarifying vision and goal setting. Some are more meticulous with it, and some may appear more chaotic, but the truth is that all high achievers are driven by vision and have created a strategy to fulfill that vision through incremental targets.

God gave me larger visions and then gave me smaller targets and strategies. I knew what I was called to do when I was about 12 years old; God has tweaked and adjusted the clarity of that vision for ministry over the years, but that has been my driving vision since my youth. Initially, as an artist, I thought being a cartoonist for Disney was my vision until God called me into ministry at a men's camp that I went to with my dad at about twelve. Narrowing the focus of my life is what propelled me forward in those visions. The Holy Spirit called my wife Katie and me down to San Diego to serve with Pastor Jurgen and Leanne Matthesius at Awaken Church in 2015. I heard God tell me he had a specific assignment for me, so I naturally answered, "What is it, Lord?" and I felt God say, "Make a million disciples." I was simultaneously excited and nervous because it felt like a lot of coffee in my future to disciple that many people. But then, as I leaned in to see how to fulfill that vision, God directed my attention to the Following Jesus book I was finishing. From there, all my focus on selling and distributing those books was fueled by the vision and mandate to make a million disciples. Many of the new books, devotionals, reading plans, and more are focused on supporting that vision. My goals and strategy to fulfill that mission are comprised of the ministry we get to do at our local church, the books and resources we release, and other platforms that God has given us. As of the original writing of this book, we're almost nine years into that vision, and we're at about 600,000 people who've been reached and discipled through the Following Jesus books and other resources! Praise God for that! God gives vision, and then he gives plans.

Budgeting

Be sure you know the condition of your flocks, give careful attention to your herds; for riches do not endure forever, and a crown is not secure for all generations.
Proverbs 27:23-24 NIV

My wife and I use a basic zero-balance budgeting strategy, which means we attempt to allocate on paper/digital in advance of the month everything we're earning, spending, saving, and giving. That way, we know exactly how much we plan to have for different areas of life. Sometimes, we use the cash-envelope strategy for periods to really focus on our stewardship of our wealth. We don't always live that way, but occasionally, we go back to the cash to tighten things up. It's kind of like my healthy eating plan. I worked with my friends Gio and Kyrsten Gonzales of Supreme Nutrition to help me budget my eating calories and macros. I then use the My Fitness Pal app to help me track my diet. It's incredible how fast it helps right the ship of my health. But I don't always use that app; I use it more in spurts to help hone in my health. Your budget tools can also work like that. They're guardrails that you use occasionally to keep you on track. Having said that, for finances, I'm more strict about sticking to my monthly budget; I just may not always use the cash envelopes.

A budget is a plan for your vision.
Wes Dunn
Pastor, Author, Investor

See budgets as a gift, not as a burden. The more aware and dialed in your budget is, the more effective you'll be in building wealth. We use the Rocket Money App for personal finances and budgeting, and QuickBooks is used for our business.

Chapter 25

Investments & Business

To build true wealth, we must move beyond just collecting paychecks to starting a business and or investing in ventures that will produce wealth. My job will add to me, but investing is what multiplies your wealth. However, to have extra to invest, you must apply the other principles in this book to increase and free up the margin to begin investing.

If you want to invest, you have to learn to live humbly. Tithe 10% and save 10% for investing.
Paul Smit
Investor & Entrepreneur

Starting A Business

Launching a business that serves and equips people is a great way to create wealth. New businesses add value to society and another income stream to your world. This section won't cover everything when it comes to business startups, but let me share a few key things to focus on. First, clarify your vision and identify your niche. Recently, we had Vance Roush speaking at our Pathfinders Business Networking Breakfast, and he said, "Don't try to be unique; try to be the only." Challenging us to work to dive deeper into solving the problem with greater clarity so that you don't have competition because you're the only one competing in your niche space. What's the unique problem that God has called you to solve? Another important note in determining what business to start is to look to your natural God design. Check out this thought from Anthony Trimino:

When considering what business to start, focus on what comes naturally to you. You'll be most effective and create most value when you do what you're good at, not just what you love.
Anthony Trimino
CEO of Traffik

Over decades of pastoring and leadership development, I've seen so many people want to do something completely outside of their calling. It's often wild that everyone but the person can see that it's not a fit, but we want to charge forward anyway. Instead of looking to start a business or service that sounds fun or interesting, ask what you're built to do. When you identify that, you'll find the business flows with more authority and success.

The final note on business ventures is to count the cost. Jesus calls a builder a fool who sets out to build a home without first considering the cost. Before you set out, take the time to flesh out the costs: start-up, overhead, staff, software, marketing, distribution, taxes, and more. Like my grandpa used to say, "Measure twice, cut once."

Investments: Stock Market

I only want to provide limited input into the trading conversation because it's not the first or primary place that I'd encourage you to start. While there can be great gains, it can also be a treacherous space while learning. Take the time to get training and coaching, or entrust your wealth to a trusted trader. I would encourage you to schedule monthly investments into the stock market just like you would do monthly deposits into your other savings and investing accounts. I'd also encourage you with the wisdom I first received on this from Jim O'Connor, which is to invest primarily in stable stock funds like the S&P 500 that aren't volatile like an individual stock. If you consistently invest in these funds over time, you'll continue to see your portfolio strengthen and multiply. Key stable funds I invest in are XLK and SPY.

Investments: Real Estate

God blessed them and said to them, "Be fruitful and increase in number; fill the earth and subdue it. Rule over the fish in the sea and the birds in the sky and over every living creature that moves on the ground."
Genesis 1:28 NIV

Year over year, Real Estate is the best long-term and appreciating investment. One of the fastest ways to increase your net worth is to move from being a renter to an owner. The first step is to secure your personal home and begin building equity. After that, begin to look for ways to leverage your current equity or other investment savings to go after other investment properties. This can be through traditional house flipping, long-term rentals, AirBNB, or syndicate investment groups.

Remember, not only is purchasing Real Estate a financial battle, but it's also a spiritual battle. Our calling to establish the Kingdom of God and push back the enemy from our land will require a fight. Each time you buy a new piece of property personally or for your business, there will be a new level of warfare. The enemy doesn't like it when the sons and daughters of God own property because that gives you and me authority. Be prayed up and ready to fight and win.

Chapter 26

Mentorship

Plans fail for lack of counsel, but with many advisers they succeed.
Proverbs 15:22 NIV

When my wife and I were stuck financially, I was invited to a business coaching event. It was an incredible event that sparked a few different next-step moments. However, one of the biggest things I felt after being in a few sessions was, "I need a coach." Why? Because I needed both *wisdom* and *accountability.* The truth is, you would be further down the track financially or in any area of your life if you knew what you needed to do to get there. There's something you don't yet know, so you're not there yet. Getting this book is a great example of getting wisdom. And I encourage you to read many more books or courses like it. A coach or mentor doesn't always need to be someone you know personally. I've been mentored in many areas of life through books and other resources from a distance.

Over the years, I've participated in both formal and informal coaching programs. I initially began being mentored in the financial area by Dr. Matt Hubbard after my wife got honest with him about where we were financially. I reached out to him and said, "Sounds like my wife talked with you." And he said, "Yes. Training starts now!" The first thing he did was recommend the book *Secrets of a Millionaire Mind* by T. Harv Ecker. Even though Ecker isn't a Christian *yet*, God used that book to break off some small thinking. I read it many times, and both Dr. Matt and I agree that it's an excellent book for communicating certain principles, which I've referenced; but there are some areas where he deviates from Biblical principles about wealth, which can be harmful. I want to draw our attention to the Biblical wealth-building principles that all successful people use, whether they acknowledge the Bible or not. I've also participated in the Life on Fire coaching program with Nick and Megan Unsworth and Dr. Matt Hubbard's Maverick Entrepreneurs coaching program. I've found that putting your financial investment into your coaching and development causes you to get the maximum out of it. It also gives you more ready access to mentors and colleagues who can help you advance in your industry. Also, it's important to note that neither of those coaching programs is unique to my area of focus in writing, ministry resources, and real estate, but wealth-building principles transcend all areas of life. I also have training and development settings for my other areas of calling.

Another primary value of coaching is accountability. Why do many people get a health coach or fitness coach? Initially, there can be some knowledge gaps, but then it shifts quickly to the discipline and accountability gaps. We usually don't need a fitness coach to teach us how to use the bench press; we need that coach to make sure we show up to use the bench press. In the same way, we engage with a business coach to teach us but even more to hold us accountable to those goals we've set. Another excellent business coaching program I recommend is the Vival Group, directed by Alex Klott. Excellent for strategic scaling of your personal life as an executive and your business.

Pride & Insecurity Block Prosperity

If mentorship is so essential, why don't we all do it? There are two main reasons: pride and insecurity. They are usually connected but easier to face separately. Pride will get you to reject the needed input for your business to thrive, saying aloud or to yourself, "I already know that." But, be honest, if you're not doing it, do you really know it? And our insecurities keep us from the right voices. Assuming that we don't belong at a particular table or that people wouldn't want to mentor you will cut you short of the desired input to grow. Here's a great suggestion: bring or send a gift to the people you desire to mentor you. It's not trying to bribe them; it's a show of honor for who they are and the value that they provide. Honor the value that you will provide in advance and watch how their calendar will open up to you.

Chapter 27

People Synergy

And Jesus grew in wisdom and stature,
and in favor with God and man.
Luke 2:52 NIV

Learning to connect with people is essential. Become a people person and learn to win the favor of other people. Since all income flows from and through people, it's imperative we learn to connect and work well with people. Ask God to continue to give you a genuine love for the uniqueness and beauty of the people in your world. Learning how to connect is critical, whether with your boss, employees, investors, or customers. Let's look at several key areas that will help us win with people.

Listening

If we're going to connect with people, we need to learn to listen well, ask questions, and engage with them. Serving and partnering with people requires growth in this area. When we first begin in business or our industry, it is more natural to be listeners and learners. As we progress in proficiency, staying open to input and feedback takes more intentionality. When you're talking with people, make sure to keep eye contact. When people see you looking away, it shows a lack of value. I have to be more intentional about not starting to answer or talk before the person is done talking. I have to ensure that I'm paying close and full attention to what's being said. In the busyness of life, we don't always have the time to stop and have an in-depth conversation, so make sure you're fully engaged when connecting with people.

Communication

The primary goal in communication isn't just information transfer but connecting with people. It's about the impact you leave on people more than the details you share. Our goal should be that even if they don't remember what we said, they'll not soon forget how we made them feel. Clear and effective communication will build trust and confidence in the people you want to work with. The more they get to know you and the more you get to know them, the greater your exchange. While actions trump words, it's words that inspire action. A crucial part of evaluating your communication skills is checking the response to your words. The more effectively you connect, the more action your words will create. This is true from public speaking and preaching to marketing and advertising. If you're a leader, your communication is even more critical. For preachers, I've written a specific book called *Preaching With Authority* that you can check out for a deeper dive into preaching and teaching.

Discernment

Working with people will require discernment about the kind of people they are. Yes, it’s vital to know when you’re dealing with difficult people, but it's even more important to learn to work well with the good people you’re connected with. For example, use the evaluations from the *five love languages*, strengths finder, or similar books to better understand the people you’re working with. While I don’t necessarily need to pander to every element of someone's relational preferences, the more I can be aware of them, the more likely I'll make genuine connections that will benefit them and myself.

A significant part of discernment is being able to read people and their choices well and often in advance to better lead and navigate the relationship. Usually, we’ll begin to see patterns in people and be able to see trouble from further away. Having said that, I’d like to encourage us to be careful not to take one snapshot of someone’s failures or difficulties; instead, remember that, just like us, people are learning and growing. I want to do my best to engage with the movie of people's lives rather than an outdated snapshot.

Compassion

One of the greatest wealth builders is learning to serve people; a key part of that will be having an empathetic perspective toward their needs. We know that resources flow toward those who solve problems. The more empathetic we are toward people, the more we can see and serve their needs. Even outside of the workplace, we win with people when we simply show care, concern, and love for people. There's depth and beauty in everyone; learn to look for it, call it out, and see it. Learn to walk with people during times of victory and defeat. Don't abandon people when they fail—care for people's whole world, not just their work. When we consider someone's marriage, kids, friends, health, and dreams, it's amazing how it unlocks the connection. As leadership authority John Maxwell says,

People don't care how much you know
until they know how much you care.
John C. Maxwell

Authenticity

There's a lie that people will lose trust when they know too much, but I've found that the more transparent and honest you are, the greater respect and authority it brings to your life. Be honest and open about what you're facing. Admit your faults and failures when needed. I'm not talking about apologizing whenever someone feels offended because that's subjective, and you can be a slave to others' feelings, but at the same time, admitting fault isn't a weakness. When you repent and say you're sorry, it goes a long way in building trust with others. Your victories will help people have their own victories, but your humanity and flaws will help people truly connect to you. Bonds are built in the struggle. Authentic people and leaders are genuine and bring people close into their world. Don't live a façade of perfection; attempting to protect yourself will cause you to be disconnected from people. Let people close; will some people hurt you? Yes, but you'll live a shallow and meaningless life without bringing people into your world. Trust is worth the risk and reward.

Encourage

The tongue has the power of life and death,
and those who love it will eat its fruit.
Proverbs 18:21 NIV

Commit to making everyone's life better around you! Have you ever been around someone who leaves you more happy, encouraged, and feeling good about yourself? I have a ton of those friends. Rex and Katrina Crain are like that for Katie and me. My pastors are like that as well. You're always going to leave more full of faith than when you started the conversation. The foundational meaning of encouragement is to "put courage in." Having and staying encouraged isn't automatic; it must be imparted and received. Who can you put courage in this week? Take the time to speak words of life and hope into someone. Call out the gold and greatness in others.

Be a builder of people!

Chapter 28

Mindset Coaching

The name of the first is the Pishon; it winds through the entire land of Havilah, where there is gold. (The gold of that land is good; aromatic resin and onyx are also there.)
Genesis 2:11-12 NIV

I mentioned the Millionaire Mind book earlier. Well, one of the most important lessons I learned from that book was the concept of a money blueprint. T. Harv shares that we all have a money blueprint from which we build our wealth, just like a construction worker uses blueprints to build their home. He shares that our upbringing and experiences create this blueprint; if you don't like your current financial reality, and I didn't like where I was when reading his book, you must adjust the blueprint, or you'll keep getting the same results. It doesn't matter how much you or I wish our financial picture were different; if we don't dig down to the root of how we think about and handle money, then nothing will change. I had to break free from some poverty mentality with money. I had to stop seeing money as the enemy and see it as a gift and a tool that I could use to serve others and my family. I had to stop thinking, "I don't have enough," and start thinking, "How do I create what I need." I had to start seeing wealth and prosperity as an unlimited river rather than a limited pie. It may sound small, but one thing I was challenged to do to start thinking bigger about money was to always pay for valet when it's available. Usually, people have a limited mindset around paying for amenities and assume that's just for rich people. The truth is, it's not that expensive, and it got me out of thinking small. I still do that to this day.

It's little shifts in your financial instincts that you need to start paying attention to so that you won't repeat the mistakes of your family or past. Here's the good news: because you're reading books like this and engaging in coaching, you're changing your money blueprint. As you upgrade your blueprints, you'll begin to see your financial house built differently. In addition to asking how do I create it, it's better still to ask, "How do I serve more people?"

Think, Feel, and Act Wealthy

As we change our mindset and thinking about wealth and prosperity, we change how we act. Not only will we make decisions that create wealth, but we'll also choose to live generously, which will bring peace and fulfillment. If you think making money is wrong, you'll have a hard time making money. We must intentionally change our thinking about money if we're going to get a different result. It's also key to note how you *feel* about money. Your feelings are powerful and will guide you towards or away from wealth. You may "know" in your head that God gives us the power to create wealth, but because of past programming, you may feel bad about having money because you feel like rich people get that way because they are taking from others.

When you see and feel the impact your wealth can have in elevating the quality of people's lives, it will enhance your ability to serve others and increase your income and prosperity. God designed the economy to work best when we focus on serving others. If you continue in a serving posture, you will love others well and be generous, which will also increase the amount of money flowing toward you.

Money Thoughts

Here's a few key Biblical thoughts around wealth that will move your life towards prosperity.

1. Think Everything Belongs to God
2. Think Abundance
3. Think Kingdom
4. Think Personal Responsibility
5. Think Stewardship
6. Think Serving
7. Think Enjoyment
8. Think Impact
9. Think River
10. Think Generosity

Chapter 29

Creativity

The man who had received five bags of gold went at once and put his money to work and gained five bags more.
Matthew 25:16 NIV

How amazing is God to create a world where our economy runs best when we serve each other? The more significant problems you can solve, the greater the impact and the larger the reward. My best-selling book, *Following Jesus*, was the result of solving a problem; to be honest, I didn't realize how big of a problem it was at the time. The Following Jesus book is a gift book that churches give new Christians to help them engage God and his Word. It's now a book, course, app, and more, serving over half a million people and counting! Because that book exposed a problem I've been called to solve and connected me to a community I could serve, I've focused most of my next books on continuing to solve that problem and serve that audience. What challenges do you have right now that you can answer? If it's something you're frustrated by and need an answer for, most likely, thousands of others are facing the same challenge and maybe even millions.

Creativity is key because most challenges you face

won't have simple solutions that everyone else sees; otherwise, they wouldn't be challenges, and they wouldn't need your support. Creativity isn't about design as much as it's about learning to uniquely solve the problems in front of you. Creativity is required when you hit roadblocks and giants in the way. Most see a wall and decide it must not be God's will for me to go this way. That's what the Israelites felt when they saw the Red Sea. But God helped Moses make a way through the sea that had never been seen before. Be committed to creating a way through whatever is in front of you.

Don't take No for an answer

While some may not like the idea of you pushing past "no", I'd encourage you to default to this premise. Why? Because it's too easy to quickly move to difficult problems being impossible, but every great product, business, and invention flowed from someone not taking no for an answer. What challenges have you given up on because they were difficult? It may be time to go after solving them again, but try to tackle them from a new vantage point. Involve others, get creative, and ask God to give you wisdom to solve the problem.

Chapter 30

Discipline & Prioritize

There is a time for everything, and a season for every activity under the heavens:
Ecclesiastes 3:1 NIV

You are where your current habits and disciplines have taken you. Those who want to prosper need to learn how to discipline themselves consistently in the right direction. It's one thing to start off in the right direction, but staying and maintaining course is what separates the average from the great. If you reject discipline because it seems too difficult or not exciting, consider what my wife Katie often says: "You can either choose the pain of discipline or the pain of regret." The truth is that the cost of an undisciplined life is always far greater than the cost of discipline. One of the areas I see this is in my physical health; disciplining my diet is difficult at times, but what's even more undesirable is an unhealthy and unfit body.

If you're too lazy to commit to actions that will bring you success, then you don't really want it.

Boundaries & Priorities

For what will it profit a man if he gains the whole world, and loses his own soul?
Mark 8:36 NKJV

Much of wealth creation and business success comes from making the right choices. These choices demand boundaries that will help you keep the right things in front of you. You have to learn what to add in and what to cut out. Not everyone will understand your choices, but success requires you to choose and reject things. The key is to allow Biblical principles and convictions to guide your priorities; those priorities then govern your choices. Too many try to gain the world and lose their soul in the process because they made gods of things that were only meant to be tools.

Prioritize The Right Yes

With discipline, you pay upfront and then enjoy the great rewards. Regret, however, is delayed pain that intensifies the longer you wait. Too many choose instant gratification and later regret it. Choose Short-term pain for long-term gain. Here are three things to prioritize:

Prioritize The Right People

The greatest value on earth is people and friendships. It's key to prioritize people. Never sacrifice your friends or family on the altar of your business. Also, when choosing the right people to be around you, be sure to look for the fruit they are displaying, not just the words they are saying.

Prioritize The Right Projects

Many people put all their time into projects and work that aren't producing. There's a lot of wasted time and energy on work, business, and mission that aren't building Kingdom or aren't moving you closer to your purpose and assignment. Is there multiplication in what you're putting your hand to?

Prioritize The Right Pace

Don't let the world dictate to you a pace that takes you out of Biblical rhythms of sabbath, trust, and rest.

Put your outdoor work in order and get your fields ready; after that, build your house.
Proverbs 24:27 NIV

We must understand patience and seasons in our business and finances. Pretending we have something doesn't do us any good. Get your income streams dialed in before you buy the great home. Keep yourself planted in the right places, and you will flourish.

Chapter 31

Excellence

Do you see someone skilled in their work? They will serve before kings; they will not serve before officials of low rank.
Proverbs 22:29 NIV

The research done in Malcolm Gladwell's book The Tipping Point highlights a powerful truth. He shares that the common thread in highly decorated people in different fields is less about raw talent and more about Mastery. As a preacher, communicator, and writer, I'll have kind people comment on how gifted they feel I am or how they were helped by one of my messages or books; while I appreciate the encouragement, the truth is that it's less about some natural talent and more a result of God's anointing and the over two decades of dedication to the calling and craft of preaching and writing. I still have plenty of room for growth and improvement, but I've reached levels of mastery due to the amount of focused investment of time that I've logged in study, training, and practice. If someone says to me, "You're a natural," I just say, thank you, but it took me 10,000+ hours to become a natural. As mentioned, there is an anointing of God factor on my life for ministry, but God still gives me the responsibility to sharpen that skill and calling. One of the ways that I saw this outwork in my life that has contributed to wealth creation is in my writing. When I first started developing as a writer, I committed to posting short thoughts every day at 8 am. I did that without fail for about three years straight. I noticed that about once a year, without soliciting, I'd get a round of compliments and comments saying how my writing had leveled up. It wasn't that I had done anything new or different; it was that I was reaching mastery as I went. As a result, writing and resourcing churches and believers is now a primary driver of our passive and residual income.

What skill, calling, or ability do you have that could produce wealth and impact for you that you've been neglecting?

Your gift makes Room

A gift opens the way and ushers the giver into the presence of the great. Proverbs 18:16 NIV

Too often, people are focused on making room rather than developing their gifts. We're too focused on getting a break in our careers and not dialed in on enlarging our capacity. The greater your skill, gift, or ability, the more doors it will open.

At the end of the time set by the king to bring them into his service, the chief official presented them to Nebuchadnezzar. The king talked with them, and he found none equal to Daniel, Hananiah, Mishael and Azariah; so they entered the king's service. In every matter of

wisdom and understanding about which the king questioned them, he found them ten times better than all the magicians and enchanters in his whole kingdom.
Daniel 1:18-20 NIV

Excellence will cause you to be seen and selected above others. Excellence in your skill will cause the promotion of man; excellence in spirit will cause the promotion of heaven. And excellence is the only worthy response to God for the gifts he's given me and you. Notice it was the excellence of Caleb that set him apart and caused God to elevate and promote him.

But because my servant Caleb has a different spirit and follows me wholeheartedly, I will bring him into the land he went to, and his descendants will inherit it.
Numbers 14:24 NIV

Conclusion

When all has been heard, the end of the matter is: fear God [worship Him with awe-filled reverence, knowing that He is almighty God] and keep His commandments, for this applies to every person.
Ecclesiastes 12:13 Amplified Bible

I'm praying that the scriptures and supporting insights and experiences on my wealth creation journey have been encouraging and helpful. Our prayer is that you would continue to prosper and be in health as your soul prospers. Reminding us that God's desired prosperity truly does flow from the inside out. As you seek Him first and keep your heart connected to Him, you'll see the goodness of God in your life. After reading this book, what do you feel God speaking to you about and leading you toward? Do those things. Learn to follow the leading of The Holy Spirit. His desire is to walk with you and lead you into all truth. Can I also remind you once more to not be discouraged with the planting and watering and growing seasons of your wealth journey? It can take time for your new Biblical way of thinking and acting to produce, but when it does, it will be a tree of life to you and everyone around you. And that's the goal, that you'd receive all of the blessing of heaven's riches and in turn showcase God's nature by being a blessing to those in your world.

The Lord bless you and keep you; the Lord make his face shine on you and be gracious to you; the Lord turn his face toward you and give you peace.
Numbers 6:24-26 NIV

About The Author

Samuel is a passionate follower of Jesus, in love with his beautiful wife, Katie, and loves being a father to his two incredible girls, Mercedes and Kenzie. He and his wife are a part of the pastoral team at Awaken Church in San Diego, CA. They also serve the broader Church community through a discipleship resource called *Following Jesus* and by preaching and ministering with a prophetic edge!

To connect with Samuel and Katie

or for any ministry inquiries,

contact them at the key sites below

scan the QR code:

samueldeuth.com
followingjesusbook.com

www.ingramcontent.com/pod-product-compliance
Lightning Source LLC
LaVergne TN
LVHW022218200926
848481LV00006B/2017